영어 손자병법

Sun Tzu
THE ART OF WAR

한영번역 Lionel Giles
영한번역 이 용 재

영어 손자병법

초판 1쇄 발행 2020년 3월 25일

지 은 이   이용재
한영번역   Lionel Giles
영한번역   이용재
발 행 인   권선복
편   집   오동희
디 자 인   서보미
전 자 책   서보미
발 행 처   도서출판 행복에너지
출판등록   제315-2011-000035호
주   소   (07679) 서울특별시 강서구 화곡로 232
전   화   0505-613-6133
팩   스   0303-0799-1560
홈페이지   www.happybook.or.kr
이 메 일   ksbdata@daum.net

값 20,000원
ISBN   979-11-5602-795-9   03150

영어 손자병법

THE
ART
OF
WAR

한영번역 Lionel Giles

영한번역 이 용 재

도서
출판 행복에너지

손자병법은 2,500년이 넘는 오랜 역사를 통해서 검증되고 살아남은 고전이다. 동양은 물론 서양에서도 사랑을 받아 왔고 현대의 군인들과 기업인들에게도 널리 읽히고 있다. 이것은 손자병법에는 시대와 공간, 분야를 넘어 인간사의 모든 분야에 적용될 수 있는 근본 원리가 들어 있다는 것을 의미한다.

중국의 한 끝에 붙어 있는 베트남이 중국에 복속되지 않고 독립적으로 살아남았고 프랑스와 미국을 상대로 싸워서 지지 않은 것은 베트남 지도자들이 손자병법에 정통했기 때문이라는 평가는 널리 알려져 있다.

임진왜란 때 나라를 지켜낸 충무공 이순신 장군도 손자병법의 고수였다는 것 역시 잘 알려진 사실이다. 그러면 지금은 어떤가? 손자병법은 우리 한국 사람들에게 너무나 익숙해져 있고 따라서 누구나 안다고 생각하지만, 실제로 그 책을 제대로 읽은 사람은 많지 않다고 한다. 더구나 최근에는 학교에서 한자를 가르치지 않기 때문에 젊은 세대가 손자병법을 읽기는 더욱 어려워졌다.

　우리는 중국과 인접해서 수천 년을 살아오면서 수많은 침략과 영향을 받아 왔다. 최근에는 중국의 경제가 성장하면서 헤아릴 수 없는 갑질을 하고 있다. 그런 중국에 당하지 않고 살기 위해서는 중국을 알아야 한다. 중국을 알 수 있는 첫 번째 방법은 손자병법을 제대로 읽는 것이다. 불과 6,109자 안에 중국의 전쟁사상이 고스란히 들어 있기 때문이다.

　손자병법은 한 번 읽고 덮어 두는 책이 아니다. 항상 곁에 두고 읽으면서 뜻을 새기고 음미해야 하는 책이다. 즉 정독, 숙독이 필요한데 손자병법을 영어로 읽고 들으면 일석이조의 효과를 얻을 수 있다.

　독서백편의자현讀書百遍義自見이라는 말이 있다. '뜻이 어려운 글도 자꾸 되풀이하여 읽으면, 그 뜻을 스스로 깨우쳐 알게 된다.'는 것이다. 손자병법을 반복해서 읽으면 그 뜻을 스스로 깨우쳐 알게 될 텐데…. 그것을 영어로 읽으면 영어로 의미를 깨우치게 된다.

　통달mastery이란 한가지 분야에 깊이있게 파고듦으로써 특정분야에 대해 막힘없이 꿰뚫고 있는 상태를 말한다. 이소룡이 말했다.

"I fear not the man who has practiced 10,000 kicks once,

but I fear the man who has practiced one kick 10,000 times."

1만 가지의 발차기를 한 번씩 연습한 사람은 무서워하지 않지만 하나의 발차기를 1만 번 연습한 사람을 두려워한다는 말이다.

수백 권의 병서를 읽는 것도 좋지만 한 권의 병서에 통달하는 것도 좋은 방법이다. 수많은 영어책을 가지고 공부하는 것도 좋지만 한 권의 책을 완전히 정통하는 것은 더 좋은 방법이다.

그래서 손자병법 한자 원문에 우리말 음을 달고 영어 번역문을 연결하였다. 그리고 그 영문을 우리말로 번역하였다. 번역을 통해서 한자와 영어의 의미를 더 명료하게 이해할 수 있었고 한자와 영어실력을 높이는 데도 많은 도움이 되었다.

그리고 영어 번역본을 읽으면서 의미를 파악하는 것뿐만 아니라 원어민의 음성으로 들으면서 익히면 영어학습도 되어 일석이조의 효과를 얻을 수 있도록 하였다.

독자들이 손자병법을 영어로 읽고 들으면서 손자병법을 보다 쉽고 재미있게 접하여 전략적 사고와 함께 영어실력도 높일 수 있기를 바라는 마음 간절하다.

Practice makes perfect!

손자병법도 영어도 훈련으로 정복할 수 있다.

목차

始計

Laying Plans

계획 수립

孫子曰 : 兵者, 國之大事,
손 자 왈　　병 자　　국 지 대 사

Sun Tzu said : The art of war is of vital importance to the
State.

손자가 말했다. 병법은 국가에 매우 중대한 일이다.

死生之地, 存亡之道, 不可不察也.
사 생 지 지　　존 망 지 도　　불 가 불 찰 야

It is a matter of life and death, a road either to safety or
to ruin. Hence it is a subject of inquiry which can on no
account be neglected.

그것은 생사가 달려 있는 것이며, 나라의 안전이냐 파멸이냐가 달려 있는
길이다. 그러므로 무슨 일이 있어도 소홀히 해서는 안 되는 중요한 연구의
대상이다.

故經之以五事, 校之以計, 而索其情.
고 경 지 이 오 사   교 지 이 계   이 색 기 정

The art of war, then, is governed by five constant factors, to be taken into account in one's deliberations, when seeking to determine the conditions obtaining in the field.

그러므로, 병법은 다섯 가지의 불변 요소를 기본으로 야전에서 획득하는 조건을 결정할 때 신중하게 검토해야 한다.

一曰道, 二曰天, 三曰地, 四曰將, 五曰法.
일 왈 도   이 왈 천   삼 왈 지   사 왈 장   오 왈 법

These are: (1) The Moral Law; (2) Heaven; (3) Earth; (4) The Commander; (5) Method and discipline.

첫째는 도덕률, 둘째는 하늘, 셋째는 땅, 넷째는 지휘관, 다섯째는 제도 및 군기라 한다.

道者, 令民與上同意也, 故可與之死, 可與之生,
도 자   영 민 여 상 동 의 야   고 가 여 지 사   가 여 지 생

而不畏危也.
이 불 외 위 야

The Moral Law causes the people to be in complete accord with their ruler, so that they will follow him regardless of their lives, undismayed by any danger.

도덕률은 사람들이 통치자와 완전히 한마음이 되도록 하여 어떠한 위험에도 두려워하거나 목숨을 돌보지 않고 통치자를 따르게 할 것이다.

天者, 陰陽. 寒暑, 時制也.
천 자　음 양　한 서　시 제 야

Heaven signifies night and day, cold and heat, times and seasons.

하늘이란, 밤과 낮, 추위와 더위, 때와 계절을 의미한다.

地者, 遠近, 險易, 廣狹, 死生也.
지 자　원 근　험 이　광 협　사 생 야

Earth comprises distances, great and small; danger and security; open ground and narrow passes; the chances of life and death.

띵(지형)은 거리, 크고 작음, 위험과 안전, 광활한 지형과 좁은 통로 등 생과 사가 걸려 있는 요인을 아우른다.

將者, 智. 信. 仁. 勇. 嚴也.
장 자　지　신　인　용　엄 야

The Commander stands for the virtues of wisdom, sincerity, benevolence, courage and strictness.

지휘관(장수)은 지혜, 신뢰, 인애, 용기, 엄격 등의 덕을 갖추어야 한다.

法者, 曲制 官道 主用也.
법 자 곡 제 관 도 주 용 야

By **Method and discipline** are to be understood the marshaling of the army in its proper subdivisions, the graduations[1] of rank among the officers, the maintenance of roads by which supplies may reach the army, and the control of military expenditure[2].

제도 및 군기에 의함이란 군대를 적절하게 구분하여 통제하고, 간부들을 계급별로 분류하고, 군대에 보급품이 제공되도록 도로를 정비하며, 군사비용 지출을 통제하는 것 등으로 이해해야 한다.

凡此五者, 將莫不聞, 知之者勝, 不知者不勝.
범 차 오 자   장 막 불 문   지 지 자 승   부 지 자 불 승

These five heads should be familiar to every general: he who knows them will be victorious; he who knows them not will fail.

이상의 다섯 가지 항목은 모든 장군들에게 친숙해야 한다. 이 다섯 가지를 확실히 아는 장군은 승리할 것이고, 모르는 장군은 패배할 것이다.

----

1 arrangement in degrees, levels, or ranks.

2 consumption, cost, spending

故校之以計, 而塞其情. 曰.
고 교 지 이 계　　이 색 기 정　　왈

Therefore, in your deliberations, when seeking to determine the military conditions, let them be made the basis of a comparison, in this wise:—

그러므로 군사적인 조건을 결정하기 위해 심사숙고할 때는 다음과 같은 점들을 기초로 하여 비교해야 한다.

主孰有道
주 숙 유 도

(1) Which of the two sovereigns[3] is imbued with[4] the Moral Law?

두 군주 중에서 어느 쪽이 더 도덕률이 몸에 배어 있는가?

將孰有能
장 숙 유 능

(2) Which of the two generals has most ability?

어느 장군이 더 능력이 있는가?

----

3 군주, 통치자, 주권자, 최고 권력자

4 be imbued with: 물이 들다, 가득 차다, 몸에 배다

天地孰得
천 지 숙 득

(3) With whom lie the advantages derived from Heaven and Earth?

천시와 지리에서 오는 이점이 누구에게 있는가?

法令孰行
법 령 숙 행

(4) On which side is discipline most rigorously enforced?

어느 쪽의 기강이 가장 엄정하게 확립되어 있는가?

兵衆孰强
병 중 숙 강

(5) Which army is stronger?

어느 쪽 군대가 더 강한가?

士卒孰鍊
사 졸 숙 련

(6) On which side are officers and men more highly trained?

어느 쪽의 장병들이 더 고도로 훈련되어 있는가?

賞罰孰明
상 벌 숙 명

(7) In which army is there the greater constancy both in reward and punishment?

어느 군의 상벌이 보다 일관성 있는가?

吾以此知勝負矣.
오 이 차 지 승 부 의

By means of these seven considerations I can forecast victory or defeat.

나는 이러한 일곱 가지의 고려사항을 통하여 승리 또는 패배를 예측할 수 있다.

將聽吾計, 用之必勝, 留之.
장 청 오 계   용 지 필 승   유 지

The general that hearkens[5] to my counsel and acts upon it, will conquer: let such a one be retained in command!

나의 계책을 경청하고 이를 사용하는 장군은 승리할 것이니 그런 사람은 지휘할 수 있게 하라.

----

5 귀를 기울이다, 경청하다

將不聽吾計, 用之必敗, 去之.
장 불 청 오 계　용 지 필 패　거 지

The general that hearkens not to my counsel nor acts upon it, will suffer defeat: - let such a one be dismissed!

만약 나의 계책을 경청하지 않고 이를 사용하지 않는 장군은 패배할 것이니 그런 사람은 무시해 버려라.

計利以聽, 乃爲之勢, 以佐其外.
계 리 이 청　내 위 지 세　이 좌 기 외

While heeding the profit of my counsel, avail yourself also of any helpful circumstances over and beyond the ordinary rules.

내 계책의 이점에 귀를 기울이는 경우 모든 유리한 환경과 일반적인 규칙을 뛰어넘어서 보좌하라.

勢者, 因利而制權也.
세 자　인 리 이 제 권 야

According as circumstances are favorable, one should modify one's plans.

상황이 유리하게 돌아가면 그에 맞추어 계획을 수정해야 한다.

兵者, 詭道也.
병 자 　 궤 도 야

All warfare is based on deception.

모든 전쟁은 기만에 바탕을 둔다.

故能而示之不能, 用而示之不用, 近而視之遠,
고 능 이 시 지 불 능 　 용 이 시 지 불 용 　 근 이 시 지 원

遠而示之近.
원 이 시 지 근

Hence, when able to attack, we must seem unable; when using our forces, we must seem inactive; when we are near, we must make the enemy believe we are far away; when far away, we must make him believe we are near.

그러므로 공격할 수 있을 때는 공격할 수 없는 것처럼 보여야 하고, 우리의 힘을 사용할 때는 비활동적으로 보여야 하며, 우리가 가까이 있을 때는 적에게 우리가 멀리 있다고 믿게 만들어야 하며, 멀리 있을 때는 우리가 가까이 있다고 믿게 만들어야 한다.

利而誘之, 亂而取之,
리 이 유 지 　 난 이 취 지

Hold out baits to entice the enemy. Feign disorder, and crush him.

미끼를 던져 적을 유인하라. 무질서를 가장하고 적을 부숴라.

實而備之, 强而避之,
실 이 비 지　강 이 피 지

If he is secure at all points, be prepared for him. If he is in superior strength, evade him.

상대가 모든 면에서 확실하면 적을 대비하라. 적의 힘이 우세하면 피하라.

怒而撓之, 卑而驕之,
노 이 요 지　비 이 교 지

If your opponent is of choleric temper, seek to irritate him. Pretend to be weak, that he may grow arrogant.

상대가 다혈질이면 그를 화나게 만들 방법을 찾아라. 약한 척하여 적이 교만해지게 하라.

佚而勞之, 親而離之.
일 이 노 지　친 이 리 지

If he is taking his ease, give him no rest. If his forces are united, separate them.

상대가 쉬고 있으면 쉴 수 없게 만들어라. 적군이 단결되어 있으면 이간시켜라.

攻其無備, 出其不意,
공 기 무 비   출 기 불 의

Attack him where he is unprepared, appear where you are not expected.

적이 준비되지 않은 곳을 공격하고, 적이 예상치 못한 곳에 나타나라.

此兵家之勝, 不可先傳也.
차 병 가 지 승   불 가 선 전 야

These military devices, leading to victory, must not be divulged beforehand.

이러한 군의 기법들이 승리로 이끌게 되니 절대로 사전에 누설되어서는 안 된다.

夫未戰而廟算勝者, 得算多也.
부 미 전 이 묘 산 승 자   득 산 다 야

Now the general who wins a battle makes many calculations in his temple ere[6] the battle is fought.

전투에서 승리하는 장군은 전투가 일어나기 전에 자신의 처소에서 많은 계산을 한다.

----

6 before; prior to

未戰而廟算不勝者, 得算少也.
미 전 이 묘 산 불 승 자　득 산 소 야

The general who loses a battle makes but few calculations beforehand.

전투에서 패배하는 장군은 사전에 계산을 적게 한다.

多算勝, 少算不勝, 而況於無算乎.
다 산 승　소 산 불 승　이 황 어 무 산 호

Thus do many calculations lead to victory, and few calculations to defeat: how much more no calculation at all!

그러므로 많이 계산하면 승리하고 적게 계산하면 패배한다. 하물며 전혀 계산을 하지 않으면 어떻게 되겠는가?

吾以此觀之, 勝負見矣.
오 이 차 관 지　승 부 견 의

It is by attention to this point that I can foresee who is likely to win or lose.

이 점에 주의하면 나는 누가 승리하고 패배할 것인지를 예측할 수 있다.

作戰

Waging War

전쟁 수행

孫子曰 : 凡用兵之法, 馳車千駟, 革車千乘,
손 자 왈　　　범 용 병 지 법　　치 거 천 사　　혁 거 천 승

帶甲十萬, 千里饋糧, 則內外之費. 賓客之用,
대 갑 십 만 천 리 궤 량　　즉 내 외 지 비　　빈 객 지 용

膠漆之材, 車甲之奉, 日費千金,
교 칠 지 재　 거 갑 지 봉　 일 비 천 금

然後十萬之師擧矣.
연 후 십 만 지 사 거 의

Sun Tzu said: In the operations of war, where there are in the field a thousand swift chariots, as many heavy chariots, and a hundred thousand mail-clad soldiers, with provisions enough to carry them a thousand li, the expenditure at home and at the front, including entertainment of guests, small items such as glue and paint, and sums spent on chariots and armor, will reach the total of a thousand ounces of silver per day. Such is the cost of raising an army of 100,000 men.

손자가 말했다. 전쟁 수행에서 쾌속전차 1천 대, 중전차 1천 대, 갑옷병사 10만, 천릿길을 가는 데 충분한 식량, 방문자에 대한 향응, 아교와 페인트와 같은 소품, 수레와 전차를 포함한 본국 및 전선에서의 군사지출 등은 매일

1천 온스의 은에 이를 것이다. 그것은 10만 군사를 거병하는 비용이다.

其用戰也貴勝, 久則鈍兵挫銳,
기 용 전 야 귀 승　　구 즉 둔 병 좌 예

When you engage in actual fighting, if victory is long in coming, then men's weapons will grow dull and their ardor will be damped.

실제로 교전을 할 때 승전이 오래 걸리면 병사들의 무기는 무뎌지고 그들의 열정은 꺾일 것이다.

攻城則力屈,
공 성 즉 력 굴

If you lay siege to a town, you will exhaust your strength.

만약 도시를 포위하면 전력은 소진될 것이다.

久暴師則國用不足,
구 폭 사 즉 국 용 부 족

Again, if the campaign is protracted, the resources of the State will not be equal to the strain.

또다시 전쟁이 길어지면 국가의 자원은 그 부담이 전과 같지 않을 것이다.

夫鈍兵挫銳 屈力殫貨 則諸侯乘其弊而起,
부 둔 병 좌 예 굴 력 탄 화 즉 제 후 승 기 폐 이 기

Now, when your weapons are dulled, your ardor damped, your strength exhausted and your treasure spent, other chieftains will spring up to take advantage of your extremity.

군대가 둔해지고 사기가 꺾이고, 군대의 힘이 소진되고 재화가 소모되면 제3국이 이 폐단을 노려 침략하려 일어날 것이다.

雖有智者, 不能善其後矣.
수 유 지 자   불 능 선 기 후 의

Then no man, however wise, will be able to avert the consequences that must ensue.

그렇게 되면 아무리 지혜로운 자라 하더라도 필연적인 결과를 돌이킬 수 없을 것이다.

故兵聞拙速, 未睹巧之久也.
고 병 문 졸 속   미 도 교 지 구 야

Thus, though we have heard of stupid haste[7] in war, cleverness has never been seen associated with long

----

7   stupid haste: 준비가 다소 부족하더라도 위험을 감수하고 속전속결을 선택하는 것.

delays.

그래서 전쟁에서 다소 미흡해도 속전속결해야 한다는 말은 들었으나 오랫동안 지연하는 현명함은 본 적이 없다.

夫兵久而國利者, 未之有也.
부 병 구 이 국 리 자   미 지 유 야

There is no instance of a country having benefited from prolonged warfare.

어떤 나라든 장기전에서 이익을 봤다는 사례가 없다.

故不盡知用兵之害者, 則不能盡知用兵之利也.
고 부 진 지 용 병 지 해 자   즉 불 능 진 지 용 병 지 리 야

It is only one who is thoroughly acquainted with the evils of war that can thoroughly understand the profitable way of carrying it on.

그러므로 전쟁의 폐해를 철저하게 아는 자만이 전쟁을 유리하게 수행하는 방법을 철저히 이해할 수 있다.

善用兵者, 役不再籍, 糧不三載,
선 용 병 자   역 부 재 적   양 불 삼 재

The skillful soldier does not raise a second levy, neither are his supply-wagons loaded more than twice.

전쟁을 잘하는 군인은 재차 징집하지 않으며, 군량을 두 번 이상 싣지 않는다.

取用於國, 因糧於敵,
취 용 어 국   인 량 어 적

Bring war material with you from home, but forage on the enemy.

군용물자는 본국에서 가져가고 식량은 적에게서 빼앗아 사용한다.

故軍食可足也.
고 군 식 가 족 야

Thus the army will have food enough for its needs.

그래야 군대의 식량을 풍족하게 가질 것이다.

國之貧於師者遠輸,
국 지 빈 어 사 자 원 수

Poverty of the State exchequer causes an army to be maintained by contributions from a distance.

국가 재정의 빈곤은 군대를 장거리 수송을 통해 유지하는 데서 기인한다.

遠輸則百姓貧.
원 수 즉 백 성 빈

Contributing to maintain an army at a distance causes the people to be impoverished.

장거리 수송으로 군대를 유지하는 것은 백성들의 빈곤을 초래한다.

近於師者貴賣, 貴賣則百姓財竭,
근 어 사 자 귀 매　귀 매 즉 백 성 재 갈

On the other hand, the proximity of an army causes prices to go up; and high prices cause the people's substance to be drained away.

반면에 군대 주변에는 물가가 올라간다. 물가가 올라가면 백성들의 재산이 고갈된다.

財竭則急於丘役.
재 갈 즉 급 어 구 역

When their substance is drained away, the peasantry will be afflicted by heavy exactions.

재산이 고갈될 때는 농민들은 가혹한 세금으로 고통을 받게 될 것이다.

力屈財殫, 中原內虛於家. 百姓之費,
역 굴 재 탄　　중 원 내 허 어 가　　백 성 지 비

十去其七, 公家之費, 破軍罷馬,
십 거 기 칠　　공 가 지 비　　파 군 파 마

甲冑矢弩, 戟盾蔽櫓, 丘牛大車, 十去其六.
갑 주 시 노　　극 순 폐 노　　구 우 대 거　　십 거 기 육

With this loss of substance and exhaustion of strength,
the homes of the people will be stripped bare, and
three-tenths of their income will be dissipated; while
government expenses for broken chariots, wornout
horses, breast-plates and helmets, bows and arrows,
spears and shields, protective mantles, draught-oxen and
heavy wagons, will amount to four-tenths of its total
revenue.

재물을 잃고 힘이 소진되면 백성의 집들이 빈집이 되고, 가계 소득의 30%
가 사라진다. 한편 정부가 파괴된 전차, 소모된 군마, 갑옷, 투구, 활과 화
살, 창과 방패를 정비하는 데 드는 비용이 정부 수익의 40%에 이를 것이다.

故智將務食於敵.
고 지 장 무 식 어 적

Hence a wise general makes a point of foraging on the
enemy.

그러므로 지혜로운 장군은 식량은 반드시 적에게서 찾는다.

食敵一鐘, 當吾二十鐘, 箕秆一石, 當吾二十石.
식 적 일 종　　당 오 이 십 종　　기 간 일 석　　당 오 이 십 석

One cartload of the enemy's provisions is equivalent to
twenty of one's own, and likewise a single picul[8] of his
provender is equivalent to twenty from one's own store.

적군의 식량 1대분은 아군의 식량 20대분에 해당한다. 적의 사료 1석은 아
군 창고에 있는 사료 20석에 해당한다.

故殺敵者, 怒也, 取敵之利者, 貨也.
고 살 적 자　　노 야　　취 적 지 리 자　　화 야

Now in order to kill the enemy, our men must be roused
to anger; that there may be advantage from defeating the
enemy, they must have their rewards.

고로 적을 죽이기 위해서는 아군은 분노가 치밀어 올라야 한다. 적의 이익
을 탈취하려면 병사들에게 반드시 상을 주어야 한다.

8　1 picul≒60.48kg

故車戰, 得車十乘已上, 賞其先得者,
고 거 전　　　득 거 십 승 이 상　　　상 기 선 득 자

Therefore in chariot fighting, when ten or more chariots have been taken, those should be rewarded who took the first.

그러므로 전차전에서 적의 전차 열 대 이상을 획득하였으면 우선적으로 획득한 자에게 상을 주어야 한다.

而更其旌旗, 車雜而乘之,
이 경 기 정 기　　　거 잡 이 승 지

Our own flags should be substituted for those of the enemy, and the chariots mingled and used in conjunction with ours.

적의 깃발을 사용해서 아군의 깃발을 달고 획득한 전차들은 아군 전차에 혼합하여 사용한다.

卒善而養之,
졸 선 이 양 지

The captured soldiers should be kindly treated and kept.

사로잡힌 적의 병사들은 친절히 대해 주고 지켜 줘야 한다.

是謂勝敵而益强.
시 위 승 적 이 익 강

This is called, using the conquered foe to augment one's own strength.

이런 것을 정복한 적을 아군의 힘을 보강하는 데 쓰는 것이라 한다.

故兵貴勝, 不貴久.
고 병 귀 승   불 귀 구

In war, then, let your great object be victory, not lengthy campaigns.

그래서 전쟁에서 가장 큰 목적을 승리하는 데 있도록 하고, 장기전에 두지 말라.

故知兵之將, 民之司命, 國家安危之主也.
고 지 병 지 장   민 지 사 명   국 가 안 위 지 주 야

Thus it may be known that the leader of armies is the arbiter of the people's fate, the man on whom it depends whether the nation shall be in peace or in peril.

그러므로 군대의 지도자는 국민 운명의 결정권자라는 것을 알 수 있는데, 나라가 평화로울지 위태로울지가 바로 그에게 달려 있는 것이다.

謀攻

Attack by Stratagem

계략에 의한 공격

孫子曰 : 凡用兵之法, 全國爲上, 破國次之,
손 자 왈　　범 용 병 지 법　 전 국 위 상　 파 국 차 지

全軍爲上, 破軍次之.
전 군 위 상　 파 군 차 지

全旅爲上, 破旅次之, 全卒爲上, 破卒次之,
전 여 위 상　 파 려 차 지　 전 졸 위 상　 파 졸 차 지

全伍爲上, 破伍次之.
전 오 위 상　 파 오 차 지

Sun Tzu said : In the practical art of war, the best thing of all is to take the enemy's country whole and intact; to shatter and destroy it is not so good. So, too, it is better to recapture an army entire than to destroy it, to capture a regiment, a detachment or a company entire than to destroy them.

손자가 말했다 : 실용적인 병법에서 최고는 적국을 온전하게 접수하는 것이지 부수고 파괴하는 것은 그리 좋은 것이 아니다. 마찬가지로 적군을 파괴하는 것보다는 온전하게 잡는 것이 더 좋고, 연대도 파견대도 중대도 파괴하는 것보다 잡는 것이 더 좋다.

是故百戰百勝, 非善之善者也,
시 고 백 전 백 승　　비 선 지 선 자 야

不戰而屈人之兵, 善之善者也.
부 전 이 굴 인 지 병　　선 지 선 자 야

Hence to fight and conquer in all your battles is not supreme excellence; supreme excellence consists in breaking the enemy's resistance without fighting.

그래서 모든 전투를 싸워 정복하는 것이 최고의 탁월함은 아니다. 최고의 탁월함은 싸우지 않고 적의 저항을 깨뜨리는 데 있다.

故上兵伐謀, 其次伐交, 其次伐兵, 其下攻城.
고 상 병 벌 모　　기 차 벌 교　　기 차 벌 병　　기 하 공 성

Thus the highest form of generalship is to balk the enemy's plans; the next best is to prevent the junction of the enemy's forces; the next in order is to attack the enemy's army in the field; and the worst policy of all is to besiege walled cities.

그러므로 최상의 용병술은 적의 계획을 저지하는 것이다. 그 다음으로 좋은 것은 적의 군대들이 연합하는 것을 막는 것이다. 그 다음은 야전에서 적군을 공격하는 것이다. 모든 방책 중에서 최악은 성을 포위하는 것이다.

攻城之法爲不得已.
공 성 지 법 위 부 득 이

The rule is, not to besiege walled cities if it can possibly be avoided.

성을 공격하는 것은 피할 수만 있다면 하지 않아야 한다.

修櫓轒轀, 具器械, 三月而後成,
수 로 분 온　구 기 계　삼 월 이 후 성

距闉, 又三月而後已.
거 인　우 삼 월 이 후 이

The preparation of mantlets, movable shelters, and various implements of war, will take up three whole months; and the piling up of mounds over against the walls will take three months more.

방탄복, 이동식 대피소, 다양한 전쟁 도구를 준비하는 데 꼬박 3개월은 걸릴 것이다. 성벽에 대항하여 흙더미를 쌓는 데 또 3개월이 걸릴 것이다.

將不勝其忿, 而蟻附之, 殺士卒三分之一,
장 불 승 기 분　이 의 부 지　살 사 졸 삼 분 지 일

而城不拔者, 此攻之災也.
이 성 불 발 자　차 공 지 재 야

The general, unable to control his irritation, will launch

his men to the assault like swarming ants, with the result that one-third of his men are slain, while the town still remains untaken. Such are the disastrous effects of a siege.

장군이 분노를 이기지 못하고 병사들에게 명령해 개미처럼 성을 공격하게 하면, 그 결과 아군 병사 3분의 1이 살해되며, 그렇게 해도 성을 빼앗지 못한다면, 이것이 바로 포위작전의 처참한 결과다.

故善用兵者,
고 선 용 병 자

屈人之兵而非戰也.　拔人之城而非攻也.
굴 인 지 병 이 비 전 야　　발 인 지 성 이 비 공 야

毀人之國,　而非久也.
훼 인 지 국　　이 비 구 야

Therefore the skillful leader subdues the enemy's troops without any fighting; he captures their cities without laying siege to them; he overthrows their kingdom without lengthy operations in the field.

그러므로 능숙한 지도자는 싸우지 않고 적 부대를 굴복시킨다. 적의 성을 공격하지 않고 빼앗는다. 장시간의 전투 없이 적 왕국을 전복시킨다.

必以全爭於天下, 故兵不頓而利可全,
필 이 전 쟁 어 천 하   고 병 부 둔 이 리 가 전

此謀攻之法也.
차 모 공 지 법 야

With his forces intact he will dispute the mastery of the Empire, and thus, without losing a man, his triumph will be complete. This is the method of attacking by stratagem.

필히 자기의 군대를 온전하게 한 채로 제국의 지배를 다툰다. 그러므로 병력의 손실 없이 완전하게 승리할 것이다. 이것이 바로 책략으로 공격하는 방법이다.

故用兵之法, 十則圍之, 五則攻之, 倍則分之.
고 용 병 지 법   십 즉 위 지   오 즉 공 지   배 즉 분 지

It is the rule in war, if our forces are ten to the enemy's one, to surround him; if five to one, to attack him; if twice as numerous, to divide our army into two.

아군이 10배이면 포위하고, 5배이면 공격하고, 2배이면 아군을 둘로 나누는 것이 원칙이다.

敵則能戰之, 少則能逃之, 不若則能避之.
적 즉 능 전 지   소 즉 능 도 지   불 약 즉 능 피 지

If equally matched, we can offer battle; if slightly inferior in numbers, we can avoid the enemy; if quite unequal in every way, we can flee from him.

아군과 적이 대등하면 적과 싸울 수 있다. 적보다 수가 적으면 맞서는 것을 피할 수 있다. 모든 면에서 대등하지 못하면 적으로부터 달아나야 한다.

故小敵之堅, 大敵之擒也.
고 소 적 지 견   대 적 지 금 야

Hence, though an obstinate fight may be made by a small force, in the end it must be captured by the larger force.

그러므로 소규모의 부대로 아무리 완강하게 전투를 하여도 결국은 대부대에게 포로가 된다.

夫將者, 國之輔也. 輔周則國必強,
부 장 자   국 지 보 야   보 주 즉 국 필 강

輔隙則國必弱.
보 극 즉 국 필 약

Now the general is the bulwark of the State; if the bulwark is complete at all points; the State will be strong; if the bulwark is defective, the State will be weak.

장군은 나라의 성벽이다. 성벽이 모든 면에서 완전하면 나라가 강력할 것이고, 성벽이 흠이 있으면 나라는 약할 것이다.

故君之所以患於軍者三.
고 군 지 소 이 환 어 군 자 삼

There are three ways in which a ruler can bring misfortune upon his army.

통치자가 자기의 군에 불행을 가져올 수 있는 세 가지 요소가 있다.

不知軍之不可以進而謂之進,
부 지 군 지 불 가 이 진 이 위 지 진

不知軍之不可以退 而謂之退. 是爲縻軍.
부 지 군 지 불 가 이 퇴   이 위 지 퇴   시 위 미 군

(1) By commanding the army to advance, being ignorant of the fact that it cannot advance; or commanding the

army to retreat, being ignorant of the fact that it cannot retreat. This is called hobbling the army.

군대의 진격이 불가능하다는 사실을 무시하고 진격하라고 명령하거나 군대가 후퇴할 수 없다는 사실을 무시하고 후퇴하라고 명령하는 것이다. 이런 경우를 군대를 절름발이로 만든다고 한다.

不知三軍之事, 而同三軍之政, 則軍士惑矣.
부 지 삼 군 지 사   이 동 삼 군 지 정   즉 군 사 혹 의

(2) By attempting to govern an army in the same way as he administers a kingdom, being ignorant of the conditions which obtain in an army. This causes restlessness in the soldier's minds.

군주가 군의 사정을 무시하고 나라를 관리하는 것과 똑같은 방식으로 군을 지배하려고 하는 것이다. 이것은 병사들의 마음에 동요를 일으킨다.

不知三軍之權, 而同三軍之任, 則軍士疑矣.
부 지 삼 군 지 권   이 동 삼 군 지 임   즉 군 사 의 의

(3) By employing the officers of his army without discrimination, through ignorance of the military principle of adaptation to circumstances. This shakes the confidence of the soldiers.

군주가 상황에 따라 적응하는 군대의 원칙을 무시하고 차별 없이 군의 장교들을 운용하는 것이다. 이는 병사들의 신뢰를 흔들어 놓는다.

三軍既惑且疑，則諸侯之難至矣，是謂亂軍引勝.
삼 군 기 혹 차 의   즉 제 후 지 난 지 의   시 위 란 군 인 승

But when the army is restless and distrustful, trouble is sure to come from the other feudal princes. This is simply bringing anarchy into the army, and flinging victory away.

그러나 군대가 편안하지 않고 불신이 있으면 다른 제후들로부터 어려움을 당하는 것은 명확한 일이다. 이것은 간단하게 군에 난장판을 불러오는 것이고 승리를 팽개치는 것이다.

故知勝有五,
고 지 승 유 오

Thus we may know that there are five essentials for victory:

그래서 승리에 필수적인 다섯 가지가 있다는 것을 알 수 있다.

知可以戰與不可以戰者勝,
지 가 이 전 여 불 가 이 전 자 승

He will win who knows when to fight and when not to fight.

언제 싸워야 하는지와 언제 싸우지 않아야 하는지를 아는 자는 승리할 것이다.

識衆寡之用者勝.
식 중 과 지 용 자 승

He will win who knows how to handle both superior and inferior forces.

우수한 병력과 열등한 병력을 모두 다룰 줄 아는 자는 승리할 것이다.

上下同欲者勝,
상 하 동 욕 자 승

He will win whose army is animated by the same spirit throughout all its ranks.

모든 계급을 통괄하여 통일된 정신으로 활기찬 부대는 승리할 것이다.

以虞待不虞者勝,
이 우 대 불 우 자 승

He will win who, prepared himself, waits to take the enemy unprepared.

준비를 한 상태에서 태만한 적을 기다리면 이길 것이다.

將能而君不御者勝.
장 능 이 군 불 어 자 승

He will win who has military capacity and is not interfered with by the sovereign.

장군이 군사적인 능력이 있고 군주로부터 간섭을 받지 않으면 승리할 것이다.

此五者, 知勝之道也.
차 오 자　지 승 지 도 야

These five are the way by which we know which side will win.

이 다섯 가지가 우리가 어느 쪽이 승리할 것인가를 알 수 있는 길이다.

故曰 : 知彼知己, 百戰不殆,
고 왈　지 피 지 기　백 전 불 태

Hence the saying: If you know the enemy and know yourself, you need not fear the result of a hundred battles.

고로 적을 알고 나를 알면 백 번 싸워도 결과를 염려할 필요가 없다.

不知彼而知己, 一勝一負,
부 지 피 이 지 기　　일 승 일 부

If you know yourself but not the enemy, for every victory gained you will also suffer a defeat.

자신을 알지만 적을 모르면 승리를 하는 만큼 또한 패배로 고통을 받을 것이다.

不知彼不知己, 每戰必殆.
부 지 피 부 지 기　　매 전 필 태

If you know neither the enemy nor yourself, you will succumb in every battle.

적도 모르고 자신도 모르면 모든 전투에서 패배할 것이다.

제
4
장

軍形

Tactical Disposition
전술적 배치

孫子曰 : 昔之善戰者, 先爲不可勝, 以侍敵之可勝.
손 자 왈   석 지 선 전 자   선 위 불 가 승   이 대 적 지 가 승

Sun Tzu said : The good fighters of old first put
themselves beyond the possibility of defeat, and then
waited for an opportunity of defeating the enemy.

손자가 말했다 : 옛 투사들은 먼저 패배할 가능성이 없도록 만전을 기하
고, 그런 연후에 적을 물리칠 수 있는 기회를 기다렸다.

不可勝在己, 可勝在敵.
불 가 승 재 기   가 승 재 적

To secure ourselves against defeat lies in our own hands,
but the opportunity of defeating the enemy is provided by
the enemy himself.

패배하지 않고 아군의 안전을 지키는 것은 우리 손에 달려 있지만 적을 무

찌르는 기회는 적에 의해서 주어지는 것이다.

故善戰者, 能爲不可勝, 不能使敵必可勝.
고 선 전 자   능 위 불 가 승   불 능 사 적 필 가 승

Thus the good fighter is able to secure himself against defeat, but cannot make certain of defeating the enemy.

그러므로 전쟁을 잘하는 자는 패배하지 않도록 자신을 지킬 수는 있지만, 적을 확실하게 패배시키는 것을 보장할 수는 없다.

故曰 : 勝可知, 而不可爲.
고 왈   승 가 지   이 불 가 위

Hence the saying: One may know how to conquer without being able to do it.

그래서 이르기를, 실제 정복할 능력이 없어도 정복하는 방법을 알 수는 있다.

不可勝者, 守也. 可勝者, 攻也.
불 가 승 자   수 야   가 승 자   공 야

Security against defeat implies defensive tactics; ability to defeat the enemy means taking the offensive.

패배에 대한 방비는 방어전술을 암시하고, 적을 패배시킬 수 있는 능력은 공세를 취하는 것을 의미한다.

守則不足, 攻則有餘.
수 즉 부 족   공 즉 유 여

Standing on the defensive indicates insufficient strength; attacking, a superabundance of strength.

방어적인 태세를 취하는 것은 힘이 충분하지 않은 것을 나타내며, 공세적인 태세를 취하는 것은 힘이 넘치기 때문이다.

善守者, 藏於九地之下. 善攻者 動於九天之上.
선 수 자   장 어 구 지 지 하   선 공 자   동 어 구 천 지 상

The general who is skilled in defense hides in the most secret recesses of the earth; he who is skilled in attack flashes forth from the topmost heights of heaven.

방어를 잘하는 자는 땅의 가장 비밀스런 곳에 숨고, 공격에 능한 자는 하늘의 가장 높은 곳에서 번개처럼 움직인다.

故能自保而全勝也.
고 능 자 보 이 전 승 야

Thus on the one hand we have ability to protect ourselves; on the other, a victory that is complete.

그러므로 한편으로는 자신을 보호할 수 있는 힘을 갖추고 다른 한편으로는 완전한 승리를 얻을 수 있는 능력을 갖춘다.

見勝不過眾人之所知, 非善之善者也.
견 승 불 과 중 인 지 소 지 비 선 지 선 자 야

To see victory only when it is within the ken of the common herd is not the acme of excellence.

승리를 예측하는 능력이 평범한 사람들의 수준에 불과하다면 최선의 승리가 아니다.

戰勝而天下曰善, 非善之善者也.
전 승 이 천 하 왈 선 비 선 지 선 자 야

Neither is it the acme of excellence if you fight and conquer and the whole Empire says, "Well done!"

싸워서 정복하고 난 다음 제국 전체가 "잘했다"고 칭찬을 한다면 그것 역시 탁월함의 절정이 아니다.

故擧秋毫, 不爲多力, 見日月, 不爲明目,
고 거 추 호 불 위 다 력 견 일 월 불 위 명 목

聞雷霆, 不爲聰耳.
문 뢰 정 불 위 총 이

To lift an autumn hair is no sign of great strength; to see the sun and moon is no sign of sharp sight; to hear the noise of thunder is no sign of a quick ear.

가벼운 털을 하나 드는 것이 힘이 세다는 뜻은 아니다. 해와 달을 본다고 해서 눈이 예리하다는 것은 아니다. 천둥소리를 들었다고 청력이 좋다는 것은 아니다.

古之所謂善戰者, 勝于易勝者也.
고 지 소 위 선 전 자   승 우 이 승 자 야

What the ancients called a clever fighter is one who not only wins, but excels in winning with ease.

예로부터 현명한 전사는 승리에 있어서 압도적인 자를 말한다.

故善戰之勝也, 無智名, 無勇功.
고 선 전 지 승 야   무 지 명   무 용 공

Hence his victories bring him neither reputation for wisdom nor credit for courage. He wins his battles by making no mistakes.

따라서 그의 승리는 명예로운 이름도 없고 용맹한 공적도 없다. 그는 하나의 착오 없이 전투에서 이긴다.

故其戰勝不忒, 不忒者, 其所措必勝, 勝已敗者也.
고 기 전 승 불 특   불 특 자   기 소 조 필 승   승 이 패 자 야

Making no mistakes is what establishes the certainty of victory, for it means conquering an enemy that is already defeated.

착오가 없다는 것은 미리 조치를 해두어 필히 승리할 상황을 만들어 놓고 이미 패배할 수밖에 없는 적을 상대하여 승리한 것이다.

故善戰者, 立於不敗之地, 而不失敵之敗也.
고 선 전 자　　입 어 불 패 지 지　　이 불 실 적 지 패 야

Hence the skillful fighter puts himself into a position which makes defeat impossible, and does not miss the moment for defeating the enemy.

그러므로 훌륭한 전사는 패배할 수 없는 위치에 자리를 잡고, 적을 패배시킬 수 있는 기회를 놓치지 않는다.

是故勝兵先勝, 而後求戰 敗兵先戰, 而後求勝.
시 고 승 병 선 승　　이 후 구 전　　패 병 선 전　　이 후 구 승

Thus it is that in war the victorious strategist only seeks battle after the victory has been won, whereas he who is destined to defeat first fights and afterwards looks for victory.

그러므로 승리하는 전략가는 이미 승리를 거둔 후에 전투를 한다. 반면에 패배하게 되어 있는 군대는 먼저 전쟁을 일으키고 이후에 승리를 구한다.

善用兵者, 修道而保法, 故能爲勝敗之政.
선 용 병 자　　수 도 이 보 법　　고 능 위 승 패 지 정

The consummate leader cultivates the moral law, and strictly adheres to method and discipline; thus it is in his power to control success.

고도로 능숙한 리더는 도덕률을 잘 함양하고 제도와 군기를 철저하게 확립한다. 그것이 성공을 통제하는 힘이다.

兵法, 一曰度, 二曰量, 三曰數, 四曰稱, 五曰勝.
병 법　일 왈 도　이 왈 량　삼 왈 수　사 왈 칭　오 왈 승

In respect of military method, we have, firstly, Measurement; secondly, Estimation of quantity; thirdly, Calculation; fourthly, Balancing of chances; fifthly, Victory.

군의 제도에서 다섯 가지 요소는 첫째 측정, 둘째 계량, 셋째 수의 계산, 넷째 균형, 다섯째 승리이다.

地生度, 度生量, 量生數, 數生稱, 稱生勝.
지 생 도　도 생 량　양 생 수　수 생 칭　칭 생 승

Measurement owes its existence to Earth; Estimation of quantity to Measurement; Calculation to Estimation of quantity; Balancing of chances to Calculation; and Victory to Balancing of chances.

지형에 따라 측정하고, 측정한 수치에 따라 계량하고, 양에 따라 수를 산출한다. 수의 산출에 따라 전력의 우위가 결정된다. 전력의 우위로써 승리가 결정된다.

故勝兵若以鎰稱銖, 敗兵若以銖稱鎰.
고 승 병 약 이 일 칭 수   패 병 약 이 수 칭 일

A victorious army opposed to a routed one, is as a pound's weight placed in the scale against a single grain. A defeated army is like a gram compared to a pound.

무질서한 부대와 맞서 승리한 군대는 저울 위에 올려진 곡물 한 알의 반대편에 올려놓은 1파운드짜리 저울추와 같다. 패배하는 군대는 무거운 추를 상대하는 가벼운 저울추와 같다.

勝者之戰民也, 若決積水於千仞 之溪者, 形也.
승 자 지 전 민 야   약 결 적 수 어 천 인   지 계 자   형 야

The onrush of a conquering force is like the bursting of pent-up waters into a chasm a thousand fathoms deep[9].

승리하는 부대의 진격은 골짜기에 갇힌 물을 천 길 깊은 골짜기에 쏟아붓는 것과 같다.

----

9 When the victorious get their people to go to battle as if they were directing a massive flood of water into a deep canyon, this is a matter of formation. (Thomas Cleary 번역)

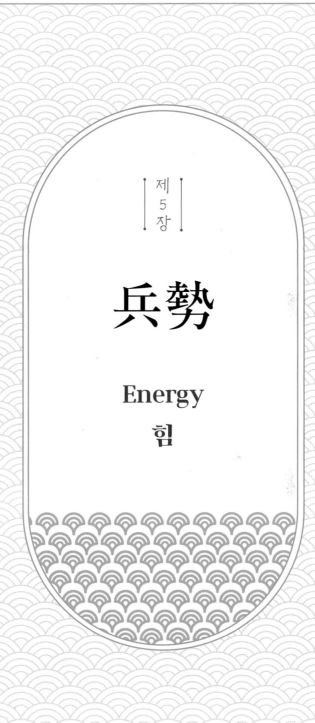

제
5
장

兵勢

Energy

힘

孫子曰 : 凡治衆如治寡, 分數是也.
손 자 왈　　범 치 중 여 치 과　 분 수 시 야.

Sun Tzu said : The control of a large force is the same principle as the control of a few men: it is merely a question of dividing up their numbers.

손자가 말했다 : 대부대를 통제하는 것은 적은 병력을 통제하는 것과 같은 원리로, 병력 수를 분리하여 통치해야 한다.

闘衆如闘寡, 形名是也,
투 중 여 투 과　 형 명 시 야

Fighting with a large army under your command is nowise different from fighting with a small one: it is merely a question of instituting signs and signals.

대규모 부대와 소규모 부대의 전투는 전혀 다른 것이 아니다. 단지 신호와 표시를 달리 조작하는 것일 뿐이다.

三軍之衆, 可使必受敵而無敗者, 奇正是也.
삼 군 지 중　가 사 필 수 적 이 무 패 자　기 정 시 야

To ensure that your whole host may withstand the brunt of the enemy's attack and remain unshaken - this is effected by maneuvers direct and indirect.

부대 전체가 적 공격의 예봉을 견뎌 내고 흔들림이 없도록 하는 것은 직간 접적으로 이루어지는 교묘한 술책에 의해 좌우된다.

兵之所加, 如以碫投卵者, 虛實是也.
병 지 소 가　여 이 하 투 란 자　허 실 시 야

That the impact of your army may be like a grindstone dashed against an egg - this is effected by the science of weak points and strong.

군대의 힘이 계란을 치는 숫돌 같으려면 약점과 강점을 잘 알고 있어야 한다.

凡戰者, 以正合, 以奇勝.
범 전 자　이 정 합　이 기 승

In all fighting, the direct method may be used for joining battle, but indirect methods will be needed in order to secure victory.

모든 싸움에 있어서 정석적인 방법이 전투를 시작하는 데 사용될 수 있지 만, 승리를 확보하는 데는 변칙적인 방법들이 필요할 것이다.

故善出奇者，　無窮如天地，　不竭如江河，
고 선 출 기 자　　무 궁 여 천 지　　불 갈 여 강 하

終而復始，日月是也.
종 이 부 시　일 월 시 야

死而復生，四時是也.
사 이 부 생　사 시 시 야

Indirect tactics, efficiently applied, are inexhaustible as Heaven and Earth, unending as the flow of rivers and streams; like the sun and moon, they end but to begin anew; like the four seasons, they pass away to return once more.

그러므로 효율적으로 응용된 변칙은 하늘과 땅처럼 무궁무진하며, 강이나 시내의 흐름처럼 끝이 나지 않고, 해와 달처럼 한 번 끝나도 다시 시작한다. 사계절처럼 사망한 것처럼 보이다가도 다시 살아난다.

聲不過五，五聲之變，不可勝聽也.
성 불 과 오　오 성 지 변　불 가 승 청 야

There are not more than five musical notes, yet the combinations of these five give rise to more melodies than can ever be heard.

음표에는 다섯 가지 이상은 없지만 그 다섯 가지의 조합은 다 들을 수 없을 만큼 많은 멜로디를 만들어 낸다.

色不過五, 五色之變, 不可勝觀也.
색 불 과 오　　오 색 지 변　　불 가 승 관 야

There are not more than five primary colors (blue, yellow, red, white, and black), yet in combination they produce more hues than can ever been seen.

기본 색상은 다섯 가지(파랑, 노랑, 빨강, 흰색, 검정)에 불과하지만 그것들의 조합은 다 볼 수 없을 만큼 많은 색조를 만들어 낸다.

味不過五, 五味之變, 不可勝嘗也.
미 불 과 오　　오 미 지 변　　불 가 승 상 야

There are not more than five cardinal tastes (sour, acrid, salt, sweet, bitter), yet combinations of them yield more flavors than can ever be tasted.

기본 맛은 다섯 가지(신맛, 매운맛, 짠맛, 단맛, 쓴맛)에 불과하지만, 이것들의 조합은 다 맛볼 수 없을 만큼 많은 맛을 만들어 낸다.

戰勢不過奇正, 奇正之變, 不可勝窮也.
전 세 불 과 기 정　　기 정 지 변　　불 가 승 궁 야

In battle, there are not more than two methods of attack - the direct and the indirect; yet these two in combination give rise to an endless series of maneuvers.

전투에서 공격의 방법에는 원칙과 변칙 두 가지밖에 없지만 이 두 가지를 결합하여 끝없는 책략을 만들어 낸다.

奇正相生, 如循環之無端, 孰能窮之哉
기 정 상 생　　여 순 환 지 무 단　　숙 능 궁 지 재

The direct and the indirect lead on to each other in turn.
It is like moving in a circle - you never come to an end.
Who can exhaust the possibilities of their combination?

전략들은 차례로 서로 연결된다. 그것은 원 안에서 움직이는 것과 같이 결코 끝나지 않는다. 어느 누가 그것들의 가능한 조합을 다해볼 수 있겠는가?

激水之疾, 至於漂石者, 勢也.
격 수 지 질　　지 어 표 석 자　　세 야

The onset of troops is like the rush of a torrent which
will even roll stones along in its course.

병력의 진격은 급류의 돌진과 같으며 그 물길에서 돌조차 굴려 띄울 수 있을 것이다.

鷙鳥之疾, 至於毀折者, 節也.
지 조 지 질　　지 어 훼 절 자　　절 야

The quality of decision is like the well-timed swoop of a
falcon which enables it to strike and destroy its victim.

굳게 마음먹은 결심의 효과는 독수리가 먹잇감을 공격하고 파괴하기 위해 질풍처럼 급강하하는 것에 버금간다.

是故善戰者, 其勢險, 其節短.
시 고 선 전 자   기 세 험   기 절 단

Therefore the good fighter will be terrible in his onset,
and prompt in his decision.

그래서 훌륭한 전사는 진격할 때의 기세는 무시무시할 것이고 결정에는 신
속할 것이다.

勢如張弩, 節如發機.
세 여 장 노   절 여 발 기

Energy may be likened to the bending of a crossbow;
decision, to the releasing of a trigger.

세(勢)는 잡아당긴 활에 비유될 수 있고 결단은 방아쇠를 당기는 것과 같다.

紛紛紜紜, 鬪亂而不可亂也.
분 분 운 운   투 란 이 불 가 난 야

Amid the turmoil and tumult of battle, there may be
seeming disorder and yet no real disorder at all.

전투의 혼란과 소동은 겉으로 보기에는 무질서해 보일 수 있지만 실제로는
전혀 무질서하지 않다.

渾渾沌沌, 形圓而不可敗也.
혼 혼 돈 돈   형 원 이 불 가 패 야

Amid confusion and chaos, your array may be without head or tail, yet it will be proof against defeat.

혼란과 혼돈 속에서 부대의 대형이 머리도 꼬리도 없게 될 수도 있지만 패배하지는 않는다.

亂生於治, 怯生於勇, 弱生於强.
난 생 어 치   겁 생 어 용   약 생 어 강

Simulated disorder postulates perfect discipline, simulated fear postulates courage; simulated weakness postulates strength.

혼돈스러운 가운데 완벽한 군기가 있고, 두려움 가운데 용기가, 나약함 가운데 강함이 있다.

治亂, 數也. 勇怯, 勢也. 强弱, 形也.
치 란   수 야   용 겁   세 야   강 약   형 야

Hiding order beneath the cloak of disorder is simply a question of subdivision; concealing courage under a show of timidity presupposes a fund of latent energy; masking strength with weakness is to be effected by tactical dispositions.

무질서의 겉옷 밑에 질서를 숨기는 것은 단지 병력수 편성의 문제이다. 소심함을 보이면서 용기를 감추는 것은 잠재적인 힘을 상정하는 것이다. 약함으로 강함을 가장하는 것은 전술적인 배치의 효과에 의한 것이다.

故善動適者, 形之,
고 선 동 적 자　　형 지

Thus one who is skillful at keeping the enemy on the move maintains deceitful appearances, according to which the enemy will act.

그러므로 적을 조종하는 데 능한 자는 적의 취할 행동에 따라 기만적인 형세를 유지한다.

適必從之, 予之,
적 필 종 지　　여 지

He sacrifices something, that the enemy may snatch at it.

뭔가를 희생시키면 적은 그것을 낚아챌 수도 있다.

適必取之, 以利動之, 以卒待之.
적 필 취 지   이 리 동 지   이 졸 대 지

By holding out baits, he keeps him on the march; then with a body of picked men he lies in wait for him.

미끼를 던짐으로써 적을 움직이게 한다. 선발된 매복조를 배치하고 적을 기다린다.

故善戰者, 求之於勢, 不責於人, 故能擇人而任勢.
고 선 전 자   구 지 어 세   불 책 어 인   고 능 택 인 이 임 세

The clever combatant looks to the effect of combined energy, and does not require too much from individuals. Hence his ability to pick out the right men and utilize combined energy.

그러므로 현명한 장군은 세를 연합한 효과를 찾지 지나치게 많은 것을 개별적인 군인에게 요구하지 않는다. 그러므로 적재를 선발하여 임명하고 연합된 기세를 활용한다.

任勢者, 其戰人也, 如轉木石,
임 세 자   기 전 인 야   여 전 목 석

When he utilizes combined energy, his fighting men become as it were like unto rolling logs or stones.

연합된 기세를 활용할 때 그 부하들은 나무나 돌이 구르는 것처럼 된다.

木石之性, 安則靜, 危則動, 方則止, 圓則行.
목 석 지 성　안 즉 정　위 즉 동　방 즉 지　원 즉 행

For it is the nature of a log or stone to remain motionless on level ground, and to move when on a slope; if four-cornered, to come to a standstill, but if round-shaped, to go rolling down.

나무나 돌의 속성은 평지에서는 미동도 없이 있고 경사진 곳에서는 움직인다. 네모난 것은 정지해 있고 둥근 것은 굴러간다.

故善戰人之勢, 如轉圓石於千仞之山者, 勢也.
고 선 전 인 지 세　여 전 원 석 어 천 인 지 산 자　세 야

Thus the energy developed by good fighting men is as the momentum of a round stone rolled down a mountain thousands of feet in height. So much on the subject of energy.

그러므로 훌륭한 장군에 의해 개발된 힘은 천 길 높은 산에서 굴러내리는 둥근 돌의 가속도와 같은 것이다. '세'라는 주제는 그렇게 중요한 것이다.

제
6
장

虛實

Weak Points and Strong

약점과 강점

孫子曰 ： 凡先處戰地而待敵者佚,
손 자 왈　　범 선 처 전 지 이 대 적 자 일

後處戰地而趨戰者勞.
후 처 전 지 이 추 전 자 로

Sun Tzu said : Whoever is first in the field and awaits the coming of the enemy, will be fresh for the fight; whoever is second in the field and has to hasten to battle will arrive exhausted.

손자가 말했다 : 전쟁터에 먼저 도착하여 오는 적을 기다리는 군대는 전투에서 왕성하고, 전장에 늦게 와서 전투를 서둘러야 하는 군대는 탈진할 것이다.

故善戰者, 致人而不致於人.
고 선 전 자　　치 인 이 불 치 어 인

Therefore the clever combatant imposes his will on the enemy, but does not allow the enemy's will to be imposed on him.

그러므로 전쟁을 잘하는 자는 적을 자신의 의지대로 통치하며, 적의 의지대로 움직이는 것을 허락하지 않는다.

能使敵人自至者, 利之也.　能使敵人不得至者,
능 사 적 인 자 지 자　　리 지 야　　능 사 적 인 부 득 지 자

害之也.
해 지 야

By holding out advantages to him, he can cause the enemy to approach of his own accord; or, by inflicting damage, he can make it impossible for the enemy to draw near.

적에게 이점을 보여주면 원하는 곳으로 적이 오도록 유인할 수 있다. 또는 적에게 손상을 가함으로써 적이 가까이 올 수 없도록 만들 수 있다.

故敵佚能勞之, 飽能飢之, 安能動之.
고 적 일 능 로 지　　포 능 기 지　　안 능 동 지

If the enemy is taking his ease, he can harass him; if well supplied with food, he can starve him out; if quietly encamped, he can force him to move.

적이 쉬고 있으면 적을 괴롭히고, 식량이 잘 지원되고 있으면 적을 굶도록 만들고, 적이 조용히 숙영하고 있으면 적이 이동하도록 강요한다.

出其所不趨, 趨其所不意.
출 기 소 불 추　　추 기 소 불 의

Appear at points which the enemy must hasten to defend; march swiftly to places where you are not expected.

적이 서둘러 방어해야 할 지점에 나타나고, 나타날 것으로 예상하지 못한 곳으로 신속히 행군하라.

行千里而不勞者, 行於無人之地也.
행 천 리 이 불 로 자　　행 어 무 인 지 지 야

An army may march great distances without distress, if it marches through country where the enemy is not.

적이 없는 곳을 통해서 행군을 하면 부대가 고통 없이 먼 거리를 행군할 수 있다.

攻而必取者, 攻其所不守也.
공 이 필 취 자　　공 기 소 불 수 야

You can be sure of succeeding in your attacks if you only attack places which are undefended.

방어되지 않는 곳만을 공격하면 공격의 성공을 보장할 수 있다.

守而必固者, 守其所不攻也.
수 이 필 고 자　수 기 소 불 공 야

You can ensure the safety of your defense if you only hold positions that cannot be attacked.

공격받을 수 없는 입장을 잡으면 수비의 안전을 보장할 수 있다.

故善攻者, 敵不知其所守. 善守者, 敵不知其所攻.
고 선 공 자　적 부 지 기 소 수　선 수 자　적 부 지 기 소 공

Hence that general is skillful in attack whose opponent does not know what to defend; and he is skillful in defense whose opponent does not know what to attack.

따라서 장군은 상대가 무엇을 방어해야 할지 모르는 공격에 능하고, 상대가 무엇을 공격해야 할지 모르는 수비에도 능하다.

微乎微乎, 至於無形, 神乎神乎, 至於無聲,
미 호 미 호　지 어 무 형　신 호 신 호　지 어 무 성

故能爲敵之司命.
고 능 위 적 지 사 명

O divine art of subtlety and secrecy! Through you we learn to be invisible, through you inaudible; and hence we can hold the enemy's fate in our hands.

절묘함과 비밀스러움의 신비한 기예여! 이를 통하여 눈에 띄지 않는 법을 배우고, 이를 통하여 들리지 않게 되는 법을 배운다. 그래서 우리는 적의 운명을 우리 손 안에 넣을 수 있다.

進而不可御者, 沖其虛也.
진 이 불 가 어 자　　충 기 허 야

退而不可追者, 速而不可及也.
퇴 이 불 가 추 자　　속 이 불 가 급 야

You may advance and be absolutely irresistible, if you make for the enemy's weak points; you may retire and be safe from pursuit if your movements are more rapid than those of the enemy.

적의 약점을 잡으면 진격할 때 절대 적이 저항할 수 없으며, 적보다 움직임이 빠르면 후퇴할 때 추격으로부터 안전할 수 있다.

故我欲戰, 敵雖高壘深溝,
고 아 욕 전　　적 수 고 루 심 구

If we wish to fight, the enemy can be forced to an engagement even though he be sheltered behind a high rampart and a deep ditch.

우리가 싸우고자 하면 적이 비록 높은 성벽 뒤나 깊은 도랑에 숨어도 교전을 강요할 수 있다.

不得不與我戰者, 攻其所必救也.
부 득 불 여 아 전 자　　공 기 소 필 구 야

All we need to do is attack some other place that he will be obliged to relieve.

우리에게 꼭 필요한 일은 적이 반드시 구해야 하는 장소를 공격하는 것이다.

我不欲戰, 雖劃地而守之, 敵不得與我戰者,
아 불 욕 전   수 획 지 이 수 지   적 부 득 여 아 전 자

If we do not wish to fight, we can prevent the enemy from engaging us even though the lines of our encampment be merely traced out on the ground.

아군이 싸우고 싶지 않으면 비록 아군의 숙영지 선이 지상에 노출되었어도 적이 우리와 교전할 수 없게 할 수 있다.

乖其所之也.
괴 기 소 지 야

All we need do is to throw something odd and unaccountable in his way.

우리에게 필요한 전부는 적이 공격할 장소를 혼란스럽게 하여 어그러뜨리는 것이다.

故形人而我無形, 則我專而敵分.
고 형 인 이 아 무 형   즉 아 전 이 적 분

By discovering the enemy's dispositions and remaining invisible ourselves, we can keep our forces concentrated, while the enemy's must be divided.

적의 진형은 찾아내고 아군은 드러나지 않게 함으로써 아군은 병력을 집중하는 한편 적의 기세는 분산해야 한다.

我專爲一, 敵分爲十,
아 전 위 일　 적 분 위 십

We can form a single united body, while the enemy must split up into fractions.

아군은 단결되는 한편 적은 여럿으로 나뉘어져야 한다.

是以十攻其一也. 則我衆而敵寡.
시 이 십 공 기 일 야　 즉 아 중 이 적 과

Hence there will be a whole pitted against separate parts of a whole, which means that we shall be many to the enemy's few.

그러므로 전체의 개별적인 부분들에 대해 균열이 생길 것이며, 이것은 우리가 적들의 소수에게 압도적인 존재가 된다는 것을 의미한다.

能以衆擊寡者, 則吾之所與戰者, 約矣.
능 이 중 격 과 자　 즉 오 지 소 여 전 자　 약 의

And if we are able thus to attack an inferior force with a superior one, our opponents will be in dire straits.

아군이 월등한 전력으로 약한 적을 공격할 수 있으면 우리의 적은 끔찍한 곤경에 처할 것이다.

吾所與戰之地, 不可知, 則敵所備者多,
오 소 여 전 지 지　　불 가 지　　즉 적 소 비 자 다

敵所備者多, 則吾之所戰者寡矣.
적 소 비 자 다　　즉 오 지 소 전 자 과 의

The spot where we intend to fight must not be made known; for then the enemy will have to prepare against a possible attack at several different points; and his forces being thus distributed in many directions, the numbers we shall have to face at any given point will be proportionately few.

아군이 싸우고자 하는 장소를 알려지지 않게 하라. 그렇게 하면 적은 공격이 가능한 다른 여러 곳들에 대해서 준비해야 할 것이다. 그러면 적이 많은 방향으로 분산되므로 특정 장소에서 아군이 맞게 되는 적의 병력은 상대적으로 적게 될 것이다.

故備前則後寡, 備後則前寡, 備左則右寡,
고 비 전 즉 후 과　　비 후 즉 전 과　　비 좌 즉 우 과

備右則左寡,
비 우 즉 좌 과

For should the enemy strengthen his van, he will weaken his rear; should he strengthen his rear, he will weaken his van; should he strengthen his left, he will weaken his right; should he strengthen his right, he will weaken his left.

적이 전방을 강화하면 후방이 약해질 것이다. 후방을 강화하면 전방이 약해질 것이다. 좌측을 강화하면 우측이 약해질 것이고 우측을 강화하면 좌측이 약해질 것이다.

無所不備, 則無所不寡.
무 소 불 비　　즉 무 소 불 과

If he sends reinforcements everywhere, he will everywhere be weak.

적이 모든 곳에 증원군을 보내면 모든 곳이 약해질 것이다.

寡者備人者也, 眾者使人備己者也.
과 자 비 인 자 야　　중 자 사 인 비 기 자 야

Numerical weakness comes from having to prepare against possible attacks; numerical strength, from compelling our adversary to make these preparations against us.

수적인 약세는 가능한 적의 모든 공격들에 대비해야 하는 데서 오고, 수적인 강세는 반대로 적이 아군에 대하여 그렇게 대비하는 데에서 비롯된다.

故知戰之地, 知戰之日, 則可千里而會戰.
고 지 전 지 지　　지 전 지 일　　즉 가 천 리 이 회 전

Knowing the place and the time of the coming battle, we may concentrate from the greatest distances in order to fight.

다가오는 전투가 벌어질 장소와 시간을 알게 되면 아군은 전투를 위하여 먼 거리에서부터 준비할 수 있다.

不知戰地, 不知戰日, 則左不能救右,
부 지 전 지　　부 지 전 일　　즉 좌 불 능 구 우

右不能救左, 前不能救後, 後不能救前,
우 불 능 구 좌　　전 불 능 구 후　　후 불 능 구 전

But if neither time nor place be known, then the left wing will be impotent to succor the right, the right equally impotent to succor the left, the van unable to relieve the rear, or the rear to support the van.

전투를 할 장소도 시간도 모르면 좌측은 우측을 지원하지 못하고, 마찬가지로 우측은 좌측을 지원하지 못하며, 전위는 후위를 지원하지 못하고 후위는 전위를 지원하지 못한다.

而況遠者數十里, 近者數里乎.
이 황 원 자 수 십 리   근 자 수 리 호

How much more so if the furthest portions of the army
are anything under a hundred li apart, and even the
nearest are separated by several li!

하물며 부대의 가장 먼 부분은 백 리나 떨어져 있고 가장 가까운 곳조차 여
러 리 떨어져 있다면 어떻겠는가?

以吾度之, 越人之兵雖多, 亦奚益於勝敗哉.
이 오 탁 지   월 인 지 병 수 다   역 해 익 어 승 패 재

Though according to my estimate the soldiers of Yue
exceed our own in number, that shall advantage them
nothing in the matter of victory.

내가 추정해 볼 때 월나라의 병력이 아군의 수보다 많다고 해도 그것이 승
리에 아무런 장점이 되지 않을 것이다.

故曰 勝可爲也. 敵雖衆, 可使無鬪.
고 왈   승 가 위 야   적 수 중   가 사 무 투

I say then that victory can be achieved. Though the
enemy be stronger in numbers, we may prevent him from
fighting.

그래서 내가 아군이 승리할 수 있다고 말하는 것이다. 적병의 수가 많다고

하더라도 우리는 적군이 우리와 싸울 수 없도록 막을 수 있다.

故策之而知得失之計,
고 책 지 이 지 득 실 지 계

Scheme so as to discover his plans and the likelihood of their success.

적의 계획과 성공 가능성을 발견하기 위해 책략을 구상하라.

作之而知動靜之理,
작 지 이 지 동 정 지 리

Rouse him, and learn the principle of his activity or inactivity.

적을 자극해서 그들이 언제 반응하고 언제 반응하지 않는지 알아내라.

形之而知死生之地,
형 지 이 지 사 생 지 지

Force him to reveal himself, so as to find out his vulnerable spots.

적이 자신을 드러내게 만들어 적의 취약점을 찾아내라.

角之而知有余不足之處.
각 지 이 지 유 여 부 족 지 처

Carefully compare the opposing army with your own, so
that you may know where strength is superabundant and
where it is deficient.

아군과 적군을 면밀하게 비교하여 어디에 전투력이 풍부하고 어디에 결함
이 있는지를 알아내라.

故形兵之極, 至於無形, 無形則深間不能窺,
고 형 병 지 극　　지 어 무 형　　무 형 즉 심 간 불 능 규

智者不能謀.
지 자 불 능 모

In making tactical dispositions, the highest pitch you can
attain is to conceal them; conceal your dispositions, and
you will be safe from the prying of the subtlest spies,
from the machinations of the wisest brains.

전술적 배치에 있어서 최고의 경지는 드러나지 않게 하는 것이다. 배치를
숨기면 간첩의 은밀한 염탐과 뛰어난 책사들의 교묘한 책략으로부터 안전
할 수 있다.

因形而錯勝於衆, 衆不能知,
인 형 이 조 승 어 중   중 불 능 지

How victory may be produced for them out of the enemy's own tactics - that is what the multitude cannot comprehend.

어떻게 적으로부터 승리를 거둘 수 있었는지 다수의 병사들은 이해할 수 없다.

人皆知我所以勝之形, 而莫知吾所以制勝之形.
인 개 지 아 소 이 승 지 형   이 막 지 오 소 이 제 승 지 형

All men can see the tactics whereby I conquer, but what none can see is the strategy out of which victory is evolved.

모든 병사들이 내가 정복하는 전술을 볼 수는 있지만 승리를 이끌어낸 전략은 아무도 알아차리지 못한다.

故其戰勝不復, 而應形於無窮.
고 기 전 승 불 부   이 응 형 어 무 궁

Do not repeat the tactics which have gained you one victory, but let your methods be regulated by the infinite variety of circumstances.

한 번 승리를 안겨준 전술은 반복해서 사용하지 마라. 끊임없는 상황의 변화에 대응하여 방법을 조정하라.

夫兵形象水, 水之形避高而趨下,
부 병 형 상 수   수 지 형 피 고 이 추 하

Military tactics are like unto water; for water in its
natural course runs away from high places and hastens
downwards.

군대의 전술은 물과 같아야 한다. 물은 속성상 높은 곳에서 낮은 곳으로 내
려간다.

兵之形, 避實而擊虛,
병 지 형   피 실 이 격 허

So in war, the way is to avoid what is strong and to strike
at what is weak.

그처럼 전쟁에서는 강한 것은 피하고 약한 것은 공격한다.

水因地而制流 兵應敵而制勝.
수 인 지 이 제 류   병 인 적 이 제 승

Water shapes its course according to the nature of the
ground over which it flows; the soldier works out his
victory in relation to the foe whom he is facing.

물은 물이 흐르는 지형의 특성에 따라 가는 방향을 정한다. 군인은 상대하
게 되는 적에 따라서 승리를 위한 방안을 모색한다.

故兵無常勢, 水無常形,
고 병 무 상 세   수 무 상 형

Therefore, just as water retains no constant shape, so in warfare there are no constant conditions.

그래서 물이 일정한 모양을 갖고 있지 않은 것과 똑같이 전쟁에서도 일정한 상황이란 존재하지 않는다.

能因敵變化而取勝者, 謂之神.
능 인 적 변 화 이 취 승 자   위 지 신

He who can modify his tactics in relation to his opponent and thereby succeed in winning, may be called a heaven-born captain.

적에 따라 전술을 조정하여 승리를 차지하는 사람은 하늘이 낸 장수라 할 수 있다.

故五行無常勝, 四時無常位,
고 오 행 무 상 승　　사 시 무 상 위

The five elements (water, fire, wood, metal, earth) are not always equally predominant; the four seasons make way for each other in turn.

다섯 가지 요소(물, 불, 나무, 쇠, 땅)가 항상 똑같이 지배적인 것은 아니다. 4계절은 순서대로 돌아간다.

日有短長, 月有死生.
일 유 단 장　　월 유 사 생

There are short days and long; the moon has its periods of waning and waxing.

낮이 짧을 때가 있고 길 때도 있고, 달은 기울 때가 있고 찰 때가 있다.

軍爭

Maneuvering

기동

孫子曰 : 凡用兵之法, 將受命於君,
손 자 왈　　범 용 병 지 법　　장 수 명 어 군

Sun Tzu said : In war, the general receives his commands from the sovereign.

손자가 말했다 : 전쟁에서 장군은 군주로부터 명령을 받는다.

合軍聚衆, 交和而舍,
합 군 취 중　　교 화 이 사

Having collected an army and concentrated his forces, he must blend and harmonize the different elements thereof before pitching his camp.

군대를 모집하고 병력을 집중시키면, 그는 숙영지를 설치하기 전에 각기 다른 요소들을 조화롭게 혼합해야 한다.

莫難於軍爭. 軍爭之難者,
막 난 어 군 쟁   군 쟁 지 난 자

After that, comes tactical maneuvering, than which there is nothing more difficult.

그런 후에 전술적 기동이 이루어지며, 그보다 더 어려운 것은 없다.

以迂爲直, 以患爲利.
이 우 위 직   이 환 위 리

The difficulty of tactical maneuvering consists in turning the devious into the direct, and misfortune into gain.

전술적 기동의 어려움은 우회하면서도 직진하는 효과를 얻어야 하고, 나의 환란을 이득으로 전환시켜야 하는 데에 있다.

故迂其途, 而誘之以利, 後人發, 先人至,
고 우 기 도   이 유 지 이 리   후 인 발   선 인 지

此知迂直之計者也.
차 지 우 직 지 계 자 야

Thus, to take a long and circuitous route, after enticing the enemy out of the way, and though starting after him, to contrive to reach the goal before him, shows knowledge of the artifice of deviation.

그러므로 멀리 돌아가는 길을 택하여 적을 유인한 다음 적보다 늦게 출발하고서도 적보다 앞서 목적지에 도착하는 것이 곧 일탈의 책략(우직지계)이다.

故軍爭爲利, 軍爭爲危.
고 군 쟁 위 리   군 쟁 위 위

Maneuvering with an army is advantageous; with an undisciplined multitude, most dangerous.

군대와 함께 기동하는 것은 유리할 수도 있고, 훈련되지 않은 많은 군중과 기동하는 것은 가장 위험할 수 있다.

舉軍而爭利, 則不及.
거 군 이 쟁 리   즉 불 급

If you set a fully equipped army in march in order to snatch an advantage, the chances are that you will be too late.

이점을 잡기 위해서 모든 장비를 갖추고 행군을 시작하면 너무 늦을 가능성이 있다.

委軍而爭利, 則輜重捐.
위 군 이 쟁 리   즉 치 중 연

On the other hand, to detach a flying column for the purpose involves the sacrifice of its baggage and stores.

반면 이점을 잡기 위해서 유격대를 파견하는 것은 군수물자에 손실을 불러올 수 있다.

是故卷甲而趨, 日夜不處, 倍道兼行,
시 고 권 갑 이 추   일 야 불 처   배 도 겸 행

百里而爭利, 則擒三將軍,
백 리 이 쟁 리   즉 금 삼 장 군

Thus, if you order your men to roll up their buff-coats, and make forced marches without halting day or night, covering double the usual distance at a stretch, doing a hundred li in order to wrest an advantage, the leaders of all your three divisions will fall into the hands of the enemy.

그러므로 부하들에게 갑옷을 걷어 올리라 명령하고, 밤낮 쉬지 않고 강행군을 하게 만들고 단번에 평소 거리의 두 배를 가고, 우위를 점하기 위해 백 리를 가도록 지시한다면, 3개 사단의 모든 지휘관이 적의 손에 넘어갈 것이다.

勁者先, 疲者後, 其法十一而至.
경 자 선   피 자 후   기 법 십 일 이 지

The stronger men will be in front, the jaded ones will fall behind, and on this plan only one-tenth of your army will reach its destination.

강한 병사들은 앞에 가지만 지친 병사들은 뒤로 쳐질 것이다. 이러한 계획으로는 겨우 부대의 십분의 일만 목적지에 도달할 것이다.

五十里而爭利, 則蹶上將軍, 其法半至.
오 십 리 이 쟁 리   즉 궐 상 장 군   기 법 반 지

If you march fifty li in order to outmaneuver the enemy, you will lose the leader of your first division, and only half your force will reach the goal.

적을 물리치기 위해서 오십 리 거리를 행군하면 첫 번째 사단의 지휘관을 잃을 것이고, 겨우 병력의 반이 목적지에 이를 것이다.

三十里而爭利, 則三分之二至.
삼 십 리 이 쟁 리   즉 삼 분 지 이 지

If you march thirty li with the same object, two-thirds of your army will arrive.

같은 목표를 위해 삼십 리를 행군하면 부대의 삼분의 이가 목적지에 도착할 것이다.

是故軍無輜重則亡, 無糧食則亡, 無委積則亡.
시 고 군 무 치 중 즉 망   무 양 식 즉 망   무 위 적 즉 망

We may take it then that an army without its baggage-train is lost; without provisions it is lost; without bases of supply it is lost.

그러므로 수송보급이 없는 군대는 졌다고 볼 수 있다. 식량이 없으면 망한다. 군수기지가 없으면 망한다.

故不知諸侯之謀者, 不能豫交.
고 부 지 제 후 지 모 자　불 능 예 교

We cannot enter into alliances until we are acquainted with the designs of our neighbors.

이웃 나라의 계획을 알게 될 때까지는 동맹을 맺을 수가 없다.

不知山林, 險阻, 沮澤之形者, 不能行軍.
부 지 산 림　험 조　저 택 지 형 자　불 능 행 군

We are not fit to lead an army on the march unless we are familiar with the face of the country - its mountains and forests, its pitfalls and precipices, its marshes and swamps.

나라의 산과 숲, 함정과 벼랑, 습지와 늪 등 지형에 익숙하지 않으면 행군에서 군대를 지휘하기에 적합하지 않다.

不用鄕導者, 不能得地利.
불 용 향 도 자　불 능 득 지 리

We shall be unable to turn natural advantage to account unless we make use of local guides.

우리가 현지의 안내자를 활용하지 않으면 자연적인 이점을 활용할 수 없게 된다.

故兵以詐立, 以利動,
고 병 이 사 립   이 리 동

In war, practice dissimulation, and you will succeed.

전쟁에서는 적을 기만하면 성공을 할 것이다.

以分合爲變者也.
이 분 합 위 변 자 야

Whether to concentrate or to divide your troops, must be decided by circumstances.

부대를 집중할지 분산할지는 상황에 따라서 결정되어야 한다.

故其疾如風, 其徐如林,
고 기 질 여 풍   기 서 여 림

Let your rapidity be that of the wind, your compactness that of the forest.

신속함은 바람과 같게 하고, 느릴때 는 숲과 같이 하라.

侵掠如火, 不動如山,
침 략 여 화   부 동 여 산

In raiding and plundering be like fire, is immovability like a mountain.

습격과 약탈은 불같이 하고 움직이지 않음은 산과 같아야 한다.

難知如陰, 動如雷霆.
난 지 여 음　　동 여 뇌 정

Let your plans be dark and impenetrable as night, and when you move, fall like a thunderbolt.

계획은 어둡게 하고 밤처럼 헤아릴 수 없게 하며 움직일 때는 벼락처럼 몰아쳐라.

掠鄕分衆, 廓地分利, 懸權而動,
약 향 분 중　　확 지 분 리　　현 권 이 동

When you plunder a countryside, let the spoil be divided amongst your men; when you capture new territory, cut it up into allotments for the benefit of the soldiery.

마을을 약탈할 때에는 약탈한 노획물은 병사들이 나눠 갖게 하고, 새로운 지역을 점령할 때는 병사들의 이익을 위해 할당량을 나눠라.

先知迂直之計者勝, 此軍爭之法也.
선 지 우 직 지 계 자 승　　차 군 쟁 지 법 야

Ponder and deliberate before you make a move. He will conquer who has learnt the artifice of deviation. Such is the art of maneuvering.

행동하기 전에 깊이 생각하고 심사숙고하라. 일탈의 책략(우직지계)을 배운 사람은 정복할 것이다. 그런 것이 '기동의 예술'이다.

軍政曰 : 言不相聞 故爲金鼓
군 정 왈　　언 불 상 문　고 위 금 고

視不相見 故爲旌旗.
시 불 상 견　고 위 정 기

The Book of Army Management says: On the field of battle, the spoken word does not carry far enough: hence the institution of gongs and drums. Nor can ordinary objects be seen clearly enough: hence the institution of banners and flags.

군정이란 병서에서 말했다. 전쟁터에서는 입으로 하는 말은 충분히 전달되지 않는다. 그래서 징과 북이 있다. 또 일반적인 사물은 선명하게 보이질 않는다. 그래서 현수막과 깃발을 사용한다.

夫金鼓旌旗者 所以一民之耳目也.
부 금 고 정 기 자　소 이 일 민 지 이 목 야

Gongs and drums, banners and flags, are means whereby the ears and eyes of the host may be focused on one particular point.

징과 북, 현수막과 깃발은 모든 눈과 귀를 하나의 특정한 곳에 집중시킬 수 있는 수단이다.

民 旣 專 一　則 勇 者 不 得 獨 進　怯 者 不 得 獨 退
민 기 전 일　　즉 용 자 부 득 독 진　　겁 자 부 득 독 퇴

此 用 衆 之 法 也.
차 용 중 지 법 야

The host thus forming a single united body, is it
impossible either for the brave to advance alone, or for
the cowardly to retreat alone. This is the art of handling
large masses of men.

단일 연합체를 이룬 군대는 용감한 자기 독단으로 진격하지 않고 겁쟁이가
독단으로 퇴각하지 않는다. 이것이 대규모의 병사들을 다루는 방법이다.

故 夜 戰 多 火 鼓　晝 戰 多 旌 旗　所 以 變 民 之 耳 目 也.
고 야 전 다 화 고　　주 전 다 정 기　　소 이 변 민 지 이 목 야

In night-fighting, then, make much use of signal-fires and
drums, and in fighting by day, of flags and banners, as a
means of influencing the ears and eyes of your army.

그래서 야간 전투에서는 봉화와 북을 많이 사용하고 주간 전투에서는 깃발
과 현수막을 많이 사용하는데, 이것은 군대의 귀와 눈에 영향을 미치기 위
한 수단이다.

故三軍可奪氣, 將軍可奪心.
고 삼 군 가 탈 기　　장 군 탈 탈 심

A whole army may be robbed of its spirit; a commander-in-chief may be robbed of his presence of mind.

군 전체가 정신을 빼앗길 수도 있다. 총사령관이 침착성을 빼앗길 수도 있다.

是故朝氣銳, 晝氣惰, 暮氣歸.
시 고 조 기 예　　주 기 타　　모 기 귀

Now a soldier's spirit is keenest in the morning; by noonday it has begun to flag; and in the evening, his mind is bent only on returning to camp.

병사의 정신은 아침에 가장 예리하다. 한낮에는 기력이 떨어지기 시작하고, 저녁때가 되면 그의 마음은 오로지 숙영지로 돌아가는 데 기울어 있다.

故善用兵者, 避其銳氣, 擊其惰歸, 此治氣者也.
고 선 용 병 자　　피 기 예 기　　격 기 타 귀　　차 치 기 자 야

A clever general, therefore, avoids an army when its spirit is keen, but attacks it when it is sluggish and inclined to return. This is the art of studying moods.

그래서 현명한 장군은 적군의 정신이 예리할 때는 피하고 적군이 늘어지고 후퇴하고 싶은 생각으로 기울어져 있을 때 공격한다. 이것이 분위기(사기)를 파악하는 방법이다.

以治待亂, 以靜待譁, 此治心者也.
이 치 대 란 이 정 대 화 차 치 심 자 야

Disciplined and calm, to await the appearance of disorder and hubbub amongst the enemy - this is the art of retaining self-possession.

군기 있고 침착하게 적군에게서 무질서와 소란스러움이 나타날 때를 기다린다. 이것이 바로 침착함을 유지하는 방법이다.

以近待遠 以佚待勞, 以飽待飢, 此治力者也.
이 근 대 원 이 일 대 로 이 포 대 기 차 치 력 자 야

To be near the goal while the enemy is still far from it, to wait at ease while the enemy is toiling and struggling, to be well-fed while the enemy is famished - this is the art of husbanding one's strength.

적이 멀리 있을 때 목표 근처에 가까이 있고, 적이 고생하고 허우적거릴 때 편안하게 쉬고, 적이 굶주릴 때 우리 병사를 잘 먹이는 것, 이것이 전투력을 절약하는 방법이다.

無邀正正之旗, 勿擊堂堂之陣, 此治變者也.
무 요 정 정 지 기　　물 격 당 당 지 진　　차 치 변 자 야

To refrain from intercepting an enemy whose banners are in perfect order, to refrain from attacking an army drawn up in calm and confident array - this is the art of studying circumstances.

깃발이 완벽하게 정렬된 적은 가로막지 않으며, 침착하고 자신감 넘치는 전열을 갖춘 군대를 공격하는 것을 삼가는 것, 이것이 상황을 파악하는 방법이다.

故用兵之法, 高陵勿向, 背丘勿逆,
고 용 병 지 법　　고 릉 물 향　　배 구 물 역

It is a military axiom not to advance uphill against the enemy, nor to oppose him when he comes downhill.

높은 곳에 있는 적을 향해 전진하지 않고, 적이 위에서 아래로 내려올 때 맞서지 않는 것은 용병의 원칙이다.

佯北勿從, 銳卒勿攻,
양 배 물 종　　예 졸 물 공

Do not pursue an enemy who simulates flight; do not attack soldiers whose temper is keen.

도망가는 척하는 적을 추격하지 마라. 열의에 넘치는 군인들을 공격하지 마라.

餌兵勿食, 歸師勿遏.
이 병 물 식　　귀 사 물 알

Do not swallow bait offered by the enemy. Do not interfere with an army that is returning home.

적이 던져놓은 미끼를 삼키지 마라. 본거지로 돌아가는 적군을 방해하지 마라.

圍師必闕, 窮寇勿迫, 此用兵之法也.
위 사 필 궐　　궁 구 물 박　　차 용 병 지 법 야

When you surround an army, leave an outlet free. Do not press a desperate foe too hard. Such is the art of warfare.

적을 포위할 때는 도망갈 길을 열어두라. 궁지에 몰린 적을 지나치게 압박하지 말라. 이것이 용병의 방법이다.

九變

Variation in Tactics

전술의 변형

孫子曰 : 凡用兵之法, 將受命於君, 合軍聚衆,
손 자 왈   범 용 병 지 법   장 수 명 어 군   합 군 취 중

Sun Tzu said : In war, the general receives his commands
from the sovereign, collects his army and concentrates his
forces.

손자가 말했다 : 전쟁에서 장군은 군주로부터 명령을 받아 부대를 소집하
고 병력을 집결한다.

圮地無舍, 衢地合交, 絕地無留,
비 지 무 사   구 지 합 교   절 지 무 류

圍地則謀, 死地則戰.
위 지 칙 모   사 지 즉 전

When in difficult country, do not encamp. In country
where high roads intersect, join hands with your allies. Do
not linger in dangerously isolated positions. In hemmed-
in situations, you must resort to stratagem. In desperate
position, you must fight.

지형이 험한 곳에는 주둔하지 말아야 한다. 넓은 길이 교차하는 지역에서는 동맹국과 손을 잡아라. 위험하게 격리된 곳에는 머무르지 마라. 갇힌 상황에서는 책략을 도모해야 한다. 절망적인 위치에서는 반드시 싸워야 한다.

塗有所不由, 軍有所不擊, 城有所不攻,
도 유 소 불 유　　　군 유 소 불 격　　　성 유 소 불 공

地有所不爭, 君命有所不受
지 유 소 부 쟁　　군 명 유 소 불 수

There are roads which must not be followed, armies which must be not attacked, towns which must be besieged, positions which must not be contested, commands of the sovereign which must not be obeyed.

가서는 안 되는 길이 있고, 공격해서는 안 되는 군대가 있고, 포위해서는 안 되는 성이 있고, 경합해서는 안 되는 지역이 있고, 군주의 명령에도 복종해서는 안 되는 것이 있다.

故將通于九變之利者, 知用兵矣.
고 장 통 우 구 변 지 리 자　　지 용 병 의

The general who thoroughly understands the advantages that accompany variation of tactics knows how to handle his troops.

전술의 다양한 변형이 가져다주는 이점을 철저히 이해하는 장군은 자기 부대를 운용할 줄을 안다.

將不通于九變之利者, 雖知地形, 不能得地之利矣.
장 불 통 우 구 변 지 리 자　수 지 지 형　불 능 득 지 지 리 의

The general who does not understand these, may be well acquainted with the configuration of the country, yet he will not be able to turn his knowledge to practical account.

이런 점을 이해하지 못하는 장군은 비록 지형을 잘 알고 있다 하더라도 그 지식을 실질적인 이익으로 전환할 수가 없다.

治兵不知九變之術, 雖知五利, 不能得人之用矣.
치 병 부 지 구 변 지 술　수 지 오 리　부 능 득 인 지 용 의

So, the student of war who is unversed in the art of war of varying his plans, even though he be acquainted with the Five Advantages, will fail to make the best use of his men.

그래서 전쟁을 배우는 사람이 자기 계획을 변경하는 기술에 능통하지 못하면 장수의 다섯 가지 덕목을 잘 알고 있어도 최선의 용병술을 행하는 데는 실패할 것이다.

是故智者之慮, 必雜于利害.
시 고 지 자 지 려　필 잡 우 리 해

Hence in the wise leader's plans, considerations of advantage and of disadvantage will be blended together.

그러므로 지혜 있는 리더의 계획에서는 이점과 손실을 함께 고려해야 할 것이다.

雜于利而務可信也,
잡 우 리 이 무 가 신 야

If our expectation of advantage be tempered in this way, we may succeed in accomplishing the essential part of our schemes.

이점에 대한 기대가 이런 식으로 조절된다면 우리 계획의 필수적인 부분을 달성하는 데 성공할 수 있다.

雜于害而患可解也.
잡 우 해 이 환 가 해 야

If, on the other hand, in the midst of difficulties we are always ready to seize an advantage, we may extricate ourselves from misfortune.

반면 고난 가운데서 우리가 항상 우위를 점할 준비가 되어 있으면, 우리 자신을 불행으로부터 구해낼 수 있다.

是故屈諸侯者以害, 役諸侯者以業, 趨諸侯者以利.
시 고 굴 제 후 자 이 해   역 제 후 자 이 업   추 제 후 자 이 리

Reduce the hostile chiefs by inflicting damage on them; and make trouble for them, and keep them constantly engaged; hold out specious allurements, and make them rush to any given point.

피해를 가함으로써 적장들을 제어하고, 그들에게 문제를 일으키고, 그들을 교전상태에 묶어두고, 그럴듯한 미끼를 던져서 특정한 곳으로 달려 나오게 하라.

故用兵之法, 無恃其不來, 恃吾有以待之;
고 용 병 지 법   무 시 기 불 래   시 오 유 이 대 야

無恃其不攻, 恃吾有所不可攻也.
무 시 기 불 공   시 오 유 소 불 가 공 야

The art of war teaches us to rely not on the likelihood of the enemy's not coming, but on our own readiness to receive him; not on the chance of his not attacking, but rather on the fact that we have made our position unassailable.

병법은 우리에게 적이 오지 않으리라고 믿어서는 안 되며, 대적할 수 있는 우리의 대비태세를 믿어야 한다는 것과, 적이 공격하지 않을 가능성이 아니라, 우리 진지를 침범할 수 없도록 대비해 놓은 사실을 믿어야 함을 가르쳐준다.

故將有五危：必死可殺, 必生可虜, 忿速可侮,
고 장 유 오 위　　필 사 가 살　　필 생 가 노　　분 속 가 모

廉潔可辱, 愛民可煩;
염 결 가 욕　　애 민 가 번

There are five dangerous faults which may affect a general:

장수에게 영향을 미칠 수 있는 다섯 가지 위험이 있다.

(1) Recklessness, which leads to destruction;

　　무모함은 파멸에 이른다.

(2) cowardice, which leads to capture;

　　비겁함은 포로가 되게 한다.

(3) a hasty temper, which can be provoked by insults;

　　급한 성격은 모욕에 의해서 분노하게 될 수 있다.

(4) a delicacy of honor which is sensitive to shame;

　　명예심에 민감한 사람은 수치를 당하기 쉽다.

(5) over-solicitude for his men, which exposes him to worry and trouble.

　　부하에 대한 지나친 배려는 걱정과 문제에 시달린다.

凡此五危, 將之過也, 用兵之災也.
범 차 오 위　　　장 지 과 야　　　용 병 지 재 야

These are the five besetting sins of a general, ruinous to the conduct of war.

이 다섯 가지는 전쟁 수행에 파멸을 초래하는 장군의 다섯 가지 죄악이다.

覆軍殺將, 必以五危, 不可不察也.
복 군 살 장　　　필 이 오 위　　　불 가 불 찰 야

When an army is overthrown and its leader slain, the cause will surely be found among these five dangerous faults. Let them be a subject of meditation.

군대가 전복되고 장수가 살해될 때 그 원인은 반드시 이 다섯 가지의 위험한 과오 중에서 발견될 것이다. 이 다섯 가지를 깊이 성찰해야 한다.

제
9
장

行軍

The Army
on the March

행군

孫子曰 : 凡處軍相敵, 絶山依谷,
손 자 왈　　　범 처 군 상 적　　절 산 의 곡

Sun Tzu said : We come now to the question of encamping the army, and observing signs of the enemy. Pass quickly over mountains, and keep in the neighborhood of valleys.

손자가 말했다 : 이제 부대의 숙영과 적의 신호를 관찰하는 문제를 다룬다. 산은 계곡에 의지하여 빠르게 넘어가라.

視生處高, 戰隆無登, 此處山之軍也.
시 생 처 고　　전 룡 무 등　　차 처 산 지 군 야

Camp in high places, facing the sun. Do not climb heights in order to fight. So much for mountain warfare.

높은 곳에 태양을 마주보고 주둔하라. 전투하기 위해서 높은 곳으로 올라가지 마라. 이것이 산악전투의 원칙이다.

絕水必遠水,
절 수 필 원 수

After crossing a river, you should get far away from it.

강을 건너고 나서는 반드시 물에서 멀리 벗어나야 한다.

客絕水而來, 勿迎之於水內, 令半濟而擊之, 利.
객 절 수 이 래　　물 영 지 어 수 내　　영 반 제 이 격 지　　리

When an invading force crosses a river in its onward march, do not advance to meet it in mid-stream. It will be best to let half the army get across, and then deliver your attack.

적군이 다가오면서 강을 건널 때는 대적하기 위해서 강 한복판으로 들어가지 마라. 적군이 반쯤 건널 때까지 놔뒀다가 공격하는 것이 최선이다.

欲戰者, 無附於水而迎客,
욕 전 자　　무 부 어 수 이 영 객

If you are anxious to fight, you should not go to meet the invader near a river which he has to cross.

전투를 하고자 할 때에 강 근처에 있는 적과 교전하기 위해 나가지 마라.

視生處高, 無迎水流, 此處水上之軍也.
시 생 처 고　무 영 수 류　차 처 수 상 지 군 야

Moor your craft higher up than the enemy, and facing the
sun. Do not move up-stream to meet the enemy. So much
for river warfare.

적보다 높고 햇볕이 잘 드는 곳에 배를 정박하라. 상류로 거슬러 오르며 적
을 대하지 마라. 이것이 강상전투의 원칙이다.

絶斥澤, 惟亟去無留,
절 척 택　유 극 거 무 류

In crossing salt-marshes, your sole concern should be to
get over them quickly, without any delay.

소택지를 건널 때는 지체 없이 빨리 건너는 데 전념해야 한다.

若交軍於斥澤之中, 必依水草,
약 교 군 어 척 택 지 중　필 의 수 초

而背衆樹, 此處斥澤之軍也.
이 배 중 수　차 처 척 택 지 군 야

If forced to fight in a salt-marsh, you should have water
and grass near you, and get your back to a clump of trees.
So much for operations in salt-marches.

소택지에서 싸울 수밖에 없는 경우에는 물과 수초 가까이 있어야 하며 숲

을 등지고 있어야 한다. 이것이 소택지 작전의 원칙이다.

平陸處易, 而右背高, 前死後生, 此處平陸之軍也.
평 륙 처 이   이 우 배 고   전 사 후 생   차 처 평 륙 지 군 야

In dry, level country, take up an easily accessible position with rising ground to your right and on your rear, so that the danger may be in front, and safety lie behind. So much for campaigning in flat country.

건조하고 평탄한 지역에서는 쉽게 접근할 수 있고 오른쪽과 뒤쪽에 둔덕이 있어서 위험은 앞에 두고 뒤가 안전한 위치를 점령하라. 이것이 평지 전투의 원칙이다.

凡此四軍之利, 黃帝之所以勝四帝也.
범 차 사 군 지 리   황 제 지 소 이 승 사 제 야

These are the four useful branches of military knowledge which enabled the Yellow Emperor to vanquish four several sovereigns.

이것이 4가지의 유용한 군사지식 분야이며 황제가 4명의 군주들을 완파할 수 있게 해주었다.

凡軍好高而惡下, 貴陽而賤陰,
범 군 호 고 이 오 하   귀 양 이 천 음

All armies prefer high ground to low and sunny places to dark.

모든 군대는 저지보다 고지를 선호하고 어둔 곳보다는 햇볕 드는 곳을 좋아한다.

養生而處實, 軍無百疾, 是謂必勝,
양 생 이 처 실   군 무 백 질   시 위 필 승

If you are careful of your men, and camp on hard ground, the army will be free from disease of every kind, and this will spell victory.

부하들을 소중히 한다면 견고한 땅에 주둔해야 한다. 그러면 모든 질병으로부터 벗어나 승리를 가져올 것이다.

丘陵堤防, 必處其陽, 而右背之. 此兵之利,
구 릉 제 방   필 처 기 양   이 우 배 지   차 병 지 리

地之助也.
지 지 조 야

When you come to a hill or a bank, occupy the sunny side, with the slope on your right rear. Thus you will at once act for the benefit of your soldiers and utilize the natural advantages of the ground.

구릉이나 제방에서는 필히 양지 쪽을 점령하여 우측 후방에 경사를 등지고 주둔한다. 그러면 병사들에게 유리하여 즉각 행동할 수 있고 지형이 주는 자연적인 이점을 활용할 수 있다.

上雨, 水沫至, 欲涉者, 待其定也.
상 우 수 말 지 욕 섭 자 대 기 정 야

When, in consequence of heavy rains up-country, a river which you wish to ford is swollen and flecked with foam, you must wait until it subsides.

상류에 많은 비가 내려 건너고자 하는 강의 수위가 오르고 거품으로 얼룩져 있으면 물이 잦아들 때까지 기다려야 한다.

凡地有絶澗, 天井, 天牢, 天羅, 天陷,
범 지 유 절 간 천 정 천 뢰 천 라 천 함

天隙, 必極去之, 勿近也.
천 극 필 극 거 지 물 근 야

Country in which there are precipitous cliffs with torrents running between, deep natural hollows, confined places, tangled thickets, quagmires and crevasses, should be left with all possible speed and not approached.

깎아지른 듯한 절벽 사이에 급류가 흐르는 지형, 천연 우물처럼 파인 곳, 뒤얽힌 덤불, 수렁과 갈라진 곳 등에서는 최대한 빠른 속도로 벗어나고 접근하지 말아야 한다.

吾遠之, 敵近之, 吾迎之, 敵背之.
오 원 지　적 근 지　오 영 지　적 배 지

While we keep away from such places, we should get the enemy to approach them; while we face them, we should let the enemy have them on his rear.

아군은 그런 곳을 멀리하면서 적은 그 근처로 가도록 유인한다. 아군은 그런 곳을 마주 보고 위치하고 적은 그곳을 등지게 만들어야 한다.

軍旁有險阻, 潢井. 葭葦,
군 방 유 험 조　황 정　가 위

山林. 翳薈. 必謹復索之, 此伏姦之所也.
산 림　예 회　필 근 부 색 지　차 복 간 지 소 야

If in the neighborhood of your camp there should be any hilly country, ponds surrounded by aquatic grass, hollow basins filled with reeds, or woods with thick undergrowth, they must be carefully routed out and searched; for these are places where men in ambush or insidious spies are likely to be lurking.

주둔지 주변에 있는 구릉지, 수초로 둘러싸인 웅덩이, 갈대로 덮인 둥그런 분지, 빽빽한 관목 숲 등은 철저히 수색해야 한다. 이런 곳들은 매복병과 은밀히 침투한 간첩들이 숨어 있을 법한 곳이기에 그렇다.

敵近而靜者, 恃其險也.
적 근 이 정 자   시 기 험 야

When the enemy is close at hand and remains quiet, he is relying on the natural strength of his position.

적이 가까이 있으면서 정숙을 유지하는 것은 적이 자기 위치가 가진 자연적 강점에 믿는 바가 있다는 것이다.

遠而挑戰者, 欲人之進也.
원 이 도 전 자   욕 인 지 진 야

When he keeps aloof and tries to provoke a battle, he is anxious for the other side to advance.

적이 거리를 두고 있으면서 전투를 도발하는 것은 상대편이 진격하기를 갈망하는 것이다.

其所居易者, 利也.
기 소 거 이 자   리 야

If his place of encampment is easy of access, he is tendering a bait.

적이 주둔하는 곳이 접근하기 쉬우면 미끼를 던지고 있는 것이다.

衆樹動者, 來也.
중 수 동 자　　래 야

Movement amongst the trees of a forest shows that the enemy is advancing.

숲의 나무들 사이에서 움직임이 보인다면 적이 전진하고 있는 것이다.

衆草多障者, 疑也.
중 초 다 장 자　　의 야

The appearance of a number of screens in the midst of thick grass means that the enemy wants to make us suspicious.

우거진 풀 가운데 많은 장애물이 나타나는 것은 적들이 아군으로 하여금 의심하게 하려는 것이다.

鳥起者, 伏也. 獸駭者, 覆也.
조 기 자　　복 야　　수 해 자　　복 야

The rising of birds in their flight is the sign of an ambuscade. Startled beasts indicate that a sudden attack is coming.

날아가던 새들이 솟아오르는 것은 매복하고 있다는 신호이다. 짐승이 놀라 움직이면 적의 갑작스런 공격이 다가옴을 뜻한다.

塵高而銳者 車來也. 卑而廣者, 徒來也.
진 고 이 예 자   거 래 야   비 이 광 자   도 래 야

When there is dust rising in a high column, it is the sign of chariots advancing; when the dust is low, but spread over a wide area, it betokens the approach of infantry.

먼지가 기둥처럼 솟아오르면 전차들이 달려가는 것이고, 먼지가 낮으면서 넓은 지역에 퍼지면 보병들의 접근을 나타내는 것이다.

散而條達者, 樵采也.
산 이 조 달 자   초 채 야

When it branches out in different directions, it shows that parties have been sent to collect firewood.

먼지가 여러 방향으로 갈라져 나가면 그것은 땔감을 모으러 분견대들을 보냈다는 의미이다.

少而往來者, 營軍也.
소 이 왕 래 자   영 군 야

A few clouds of dust moving to and fro signify that the army is encamping.

먼지가 소규모로 발생하고 왔다 갔다 하면 부대가 군영을 만드는 것을 가리킨다.

辭卑而益備者, 進也.
사 비 이 익 비 자   진 야

Humble words and increased preparations are signs that the enemy is about to advance.

적군의 언행이 공손하고 준비가 탄탄해지는 것은 적의 진격이 임박했다는 신호이다.

辭詭而强進驅者, 退也.
사 궤 이 강 진 구 자   퇴 야

Violent language and driving forward as if to the attack are signs that he will retreat.

언행이 거칠고 진격하려는 것처럼 겁주는 것은 적이 후퇴할 신호이다.

輕車先出居其側者, 陣也.
경 거 선 출 거 기 측 자   진 야

When the light chariots come out first and take up a position on the wings, it is a sign that the enemy is forming for battle.

경전차가 먼저 나와 측면에 배치되는 것은 전투를 위한 대형을 취하고 있다는 신호이다.

無約而請和者, 謀也.
무 약 이 청 화 자　모 야

Peace proposals unaccompanied by a sworn covenant indicate a plot.

확실한 약속 없이 하는 평화 제안은 음모를 나타낸다.

奔走而陳兵車者, 期也.
분 주 이 진 병 거 자　기 야

When there is much running about and the soldiers fall into rank, it means that the critical moment has come.

병사들이 분주히 돌아다니고 전차를 배치하고 있는 것은 결정적인 순간이 왔음을 의미한다.

半進半退者, 誘也.
반 진 반 퇴 자　유 야

When some are seen advancing and some retreating, it is a lure.

일부는 진격하고 일부는 후퇴하는 것이 보이면 그것은 미끼다.

仗而立者, 飢也.
장 이 립 자   기 야

When the soldiers stand leaning on their spears, they are faint from want of food.

병사들이 창에 의지하여 기대고 있다면 식량 부족으로 허덕이는 것이다.

汲而先飮者, 渴也.
급 이 선 음 자   갈 야

If those who are sent to draw water begin by drinking themselves, the army is suffering from thirst.

물을 길러 간 자들이 자기들 먼저 마시면 부대가 갈증으로 고통받고 있는 것이다.

見利而不進者, 勞也.
견 리 이 부 진 자   노 야

If the enemy sees an advantage to be gained and makes no effort to secure it, the soldiers are exhausted.

적이 얻을 수 있는 이득을 보고도 가지려고 노력하지 않는 것은 병사들이 탈진한 것이다.

鳥集者, 虛也.
조 집 자　허 야

If birds gather on any spot, it is unoccupied.

새가 모이는 곳은 비어 있는 곳이다.

夜呼者, 恐也.
야 호 자　공 야

Clamor by night betokens nervousness.

야밤에 큰소리를 내는 것은 초조함을 나타낸다.

軍擾者, 將不重也.
군 요 자　장 부 중 야

If there is disturbance in the camp, the general's authority is weak.

군영에서 소동이 발생하는 것은 장군이 권위가 약하다는 것이다.

旌旗動者, 亂也.
정 기 동 자　난 야

If the banners and flags are shifted about, sedition is afoot.

깃발이 이리저리 움직이는 것은 난동이 일어나고 있는 것이다.

吏怒者, 倦也.
이 노 자　　 권 야

If the officers are angry, it means that the men are weary.

장교들이 화를 내는 것은 병사들이 지쳐 있다는 의미이다.

殺馬肉食者, 軍無糧也. 懸缻不返其舍者, 窮寇也.
살 마 육 식 자　 군 무 양 야　　 현 부 불 반 기 사 자　　 궁 구 야

When an army feeds its horses with grain and kills its
cattle for food, and when the men do not hang their
cooking-pots over the camp-fires, showing that they will
not return to their tents, you may know that they are
determined to fight to the death.

부대가 곡식으로 말을 먹이고, 소를 잡아먹으며, 병사들이 모닥불 위에 솥
을 걸지 않으면 그들은 텐트로 돌아오지 않을 것임을 보여주는 것이며, 그
들은 죽을 때까지 싸울 결심이 섰음을 알 수 있다.

諄諄翕翕, 徐與人言者, 失衆也.
순 순 흡 흡　　 서 여 인 언 자　　 실 중 야

The sight of men whispering together in small knots or
speaking in subdued tones points to disaffection amongst
the rank and file.

병사들이 몇몇씩 모여 속삭이거나 가라앉은 어조로 이야기하는 모습은 일
반 병사들 사이에 불만이 있다는 것을 가리킨다.

數賞者, 窘也 數罰者, 困也.
삭 상 자   군 야   삭 벌 자   곤 야

Too frequent rewards signify that the enemy is at the end of his resources; too many punishments betray a condition of dire distress.

빈번한 포상은 적의 자원이 바닥났다는 것을 의미하고 빈번한 처벌은 극심하게 고통받는 상태를 드러낸다.

先暴而後畏其衆者, 不精之至也.
선 포 이 후 외 기 중 자   주 정 지 지 야

To begin by bluster, but afterwards to take fright at the enemy's numbers, shows a supreme lack of intelligence.

허장성세로 시작하고 나서 적들의 수에 놀라 두려워하는 것은 장수의 지성이 부족함을 보여준다.

來委謝者, 欲休息也.
내 위 사 자   욕 휴 식 야

When envoys are sent with compliments in their mouths, it is a sign that the enemy wishes for a truce.

사절을 보내어 칭송을 하는 것은 적이 휴전을 원한다는 신호이다.

兵怒而相迎, 久而不合, 又不相去, 必謹察之.
병 노 이 상 영   구 이 불 합   우 불 상 거   필 근 찰 지

If the enemy's troops march up angrily and remain facing ours for a long time without either joining battle or taking themselves off again, the situation is one that demands great vigilance and circumspection.

적 부대가 화를 내며 진격해 와서 아군과 오랫동안 대치하고 있으면서도 결전을 하지도 철수를 하지도 않을 때는 철저한 경계와 세심한 주의가 요구되는 상황이다.

兵非益多也, 惟無武進, 足以倂力料敵, 取人而已.
병 비 익 다 야   유 무 무 진   족 이 병 력 료 적   취 인 이 이

If our troops are no more in number than the enemy, that is amply sufficient; it only means that no direct attack can be made. What we can do is simply to concentrate all our available strength, keep a close watch on the enemy, and obtain reinforcements.

아군의 숫자가 적보다 많지 않아도 그걸로 충분하다. 그것은 단지 직접적인 공격이 불가능하다는 것을 의미할 뿐이다. 우리가 할 수 있는 것은 단지 가능한 모든 전력을 집중하고, 적을 면밀히 감시하며 증원군을 확보하는 것이다.

夫惟無慮而易敵者, 必擒於人.
부 유 무 려 이 이 적 자   필 금 어 인

He who exercises no forethought but makes light of his opponents is sure to be captured by them.

사전에 깊이 생각하지 않고 적을 가볍게 보는 자는 분명히 적에게 사로잡힌다.

卒未親附而罰之, 則不服, 不服則難用也.
졸 미 친 부 이 벌 지   즉 불 복   불 복 즉 난 용 야

If soldiers are punished before they have grown attached to you, they will not prove submissive; and, unless submissive, then will be practically useless.

병사들이 장군과 친해지기도 전에 벌을 받으면 속으로는 복종하지 않을 것이다. 복종하지 않으면 사실상 쓸모가 없다.

卒已親附而罰不行, 則不可用也.
졸 이 친 부 이 벌 불 행   즉 줄 가 용 야

If, when the soldiers have become attached to you, punishments are not enforced, they will still be useless.

병사들이 장군과 친해졌다고 해도 처벌이 집행되지 않으면, 그들은 아직도 쓸모가 없다.

故令之以文, 齊之以武, 是謂必取.
고 령 지 이 문　　제 지 이 무　　시 위 필 취

Therefore soldiers must be treated in the first instance with humanity, but kept under control by means of iron discipline. This is a certain road to victory.

그래서 병사들은 우선 인륜을 가지고 대우받아야 하지만 엄정한 군기로 통제되어야 한다. 이것이 확실하게 승리로 가는 길이다.

令素行以教其民, 則民服, 令不素行以教其民,
영 소 행 이 교 기 민　　즉 민 복　　영 불 소 행 이 교 기 민

則民不服,
즉 민 불 복

If in training soldiers commands are habitually enforced, the army will be well-disciplined; if not, its discipline will be bad.

병사들의 훈련에서 명령이 정기적으로 집행되면 그 부대는 군기가 엄정해질 것이다. 그렇지 않으면 군기는 문란해진다.

令素行者, 與衆相得也.
영 소 행 자   여 중 상 득 야

If a general shows confidence in his men but always
insists on his orders being obeyed, the gain will be mutual.

장군이 자기 부하들을 자랑스러워함을 나타내고 동시에 늘 자신의 명령에
복종할 것을 요구한다면 장군과 병사 모두 상호 간에 이익을 얻을 것이다.

地形

Terrain

지형

孫子曰 ： 地形有通者, 有挂者, 有支者,
손 자 왈　　　지 형 유 통 자　　유 괘 자　　유 지 자

有隘者, 有險者, 有遠者,
유 애 자　　유 험 자　　유 원 자

Sun Tzu said : We may distinguish six kinds of terrain, to wit:

손자가 말했다. 우리는 지형을 6가지로 구분할 수 있다. 더 정확히 말하면:

(1) Accessible ground; 통형(접근 가능한 지형)

(2) entangling ground; 괘형(뒤얽힌 지형)

(3) temporizing ground; 지형(임시 지형)

(4) narrow passes; 애형(좁은 통로)

(5) precipitous heights; 험형(험준한 산)

(6) positions at a great distance from the enemy. 원형(적과 멀리 떨어져 있는 위치) 등이다.

我可以往, 彼可以來, 曰通.
아 가 이 왕　　피 가 이 래　　왈 통

Ground which can be freely traversed by both sides is called accessible.

아군과 적군이 모두 자유롭게 가로지를 수 있는 곳이 통형이다.

通形者, 先居高陽, 利糧道, 以戰則利,
통 형 자　　선 거 고 양　　이 량 도　　이 전 즉 리

With regard to ground of this nature, be before the enemy in occupying the raised and sunny spots, and carefully guard your line of supplies. Then you will be able to fight with advantage.

이런 성격의 지형과 관련하여 적에 앞서 양지바른 고지대를 점령하고 보급로를 철저하게 경비하라. 그러면 유리한 조건을 갖고 전투를 할 수 있다.

可以往, 難以返, 曰挂.
가 이 왕　　난 이 반　　왈 괘

Ground which can be abandoned but is hard to re-occupy is called entangling.

포기할 수 있지만 다시 점령하기는 어려운 지형을 괘형(뒤얽힌 지형)이라 한다.

挂形者, 敵無備, 出而勝之, 敵若有備,
괘 형 자　적 무 비　출 이 승 지　적 약 유 비

出而不勝, 難以返, 不利.
출 이 불 승　난 이 반　불 리

From a position of this sort, if the enemy is unprepared,
you may sally forth and defeat him. But if the enemy is
prepared for your coming, and you fail to defeat him,
then, return being impossible, disaster will ensue.

이런 종류의 지형에서 적이 준비되어 있지 않다면 나아가 적을 쳐부숴야
한다. 그러나 적이 아군이 올 것에 대한 준비가 되어 있어서 적을 격파하는
데 실패한다면, 후퇴가 불가능하여 재앙이 뒤따를 것이다.

我出而不利, 彼出而不利, 曰支.
아 출 이 불 리　피 출 이 불 리　왈 지

When the position is such that neither side will gain by
making the first move, it is called temporizing ground.

아군이든 적군이든 어느 쪽도 먼저 움직여서 득이 되지 않는 곳을 지형(支
形, 임시 지형)이라 한다.

支形者, 敵雖利我, 我無出也, 引而去之,
지 형 자 적 수 리 아 아 무 출 야 인 이 거 지

令敵半出而擊之, 利.
영 적 반 출 이 격 지   리

In a position of this sort, even though the enemy should offer us an attractive bait, it will be advisable not to stir forth, but rather to retreat, thus enticing the enemy in his turn; then, when part of his army has come out, we may deliver our attack with advantage.

이런 종류의 지형에서는 적이 아군에게 매혹적인 미끼를 던져도 출격하는 것보다 후퇴하여 적을 유인하는 것이 바람직하다. 그리고 나서 적의 일부가 나왔을 때, 유리한 입장에서 공격할 수 있다.

隘形者, 我先居之, 必盈之以待敵.
애 형 자 아 선 거 지 필 영 지 이 대 적

With regard to narrow passes, if you can occupy them first, let them be strongly garrisoned and await the advent of the enemy.

좁은 통로인 애형을 아군이 선점할 수 있다면 주둔지를 강력하게 구축하고 적의 출현을 기다려라.

若敵先居之, 盈而勿從, 不盈而從之.
약 적 선 거 지　영 이 물 종　불 영 이 종 지

Should the army forestall you in occupying a pass, do not go after him if the pass is fully garrisoned, but only if it is weakly garrisoned.

만약 적이 아군의 통로 점령을 방해하는 경우, 주둔지가 잘 구축되어 있으면 추격하지 말고 경계가 약할 때만 격파한다.

險形者, 我先居之, 必居高陽以待敵.
험 형 자　아 선 거 지　필 거 고 양 이 대 적

With regard to precipitous heights, if you are beforehand with your adversary, you should occupy the raised and sunny spots, and there wait for him to come up.

험형(험준한 산)에서는 아군이 적보다 먼저 점령하면 해가 잘 드는 고지를 점령하고 거기서 적이 오기를 기다린다.

若敵先居之, 引而去之, 勿從也.
약 적 선 거 지　인 이 거 지　물 종 야

If the enemy has occupied them before you, do not follow him, but retreat and try to entice him away.

그런 곳을 적이 먼저 점령하면 따라가지 말고 뒤로 물러나 적을 유인해 낸다.

遠形者, 勢均, 難以挑戰, 戰而不利.
원 형 자　세 균　난 이 도 전　전 이 불 리

If you are situated at a great distance from the enemy, and the strength of the two armies is equal, it is not easy to provoke a battle, and fighting will be to your disadvantage.

적이 먼 거리에 위치해 있으며 피아간의 전투력이 동일할 때는, 싸움을 걸기가 쉽지 않고, 전투가 아군에게 불리하게 작용할 것이다.

凡此六者, 地之道也, 將之至任, 不可不察也.
범 차 육 자　지 지 도 야　장 지 지 임　불 가 불 찰 야

These six are the principles connected with Earth. The general who has attained a responsible post must be careful to study them.

이런 여섯 가지가 지형과 연결되어 있는 원칙이다. 책임 있는 직책을 소유한 장군은 반드시 이 원칙들을 철저하게 연구해야 한다.

故兵有走者, 有弛者, 有陷者, 有崩者, 有亂者,
고 병 유 주 자　유 이 자　유 함 자　유 붕 자　유 난 자

有北者.
유 배 자

凡此六者, 非天之災, 將之過也.
범 차 육 자　비 천 지 재　장 지 과 야

Now an army is exposed to six several calamities, not arising from natural causes, but from faults for which the general is responsible. These are: (1) Flight; (2) insubordination; (3) collapse; (4) ruin; (5) disorganization; (6) rout.

군대는 여섯 가지의 재앙에 빠질 위험에 노출되어 있는데 이것들은 자연적인 원인에 의한 것이 아니라 군을 책임지고 있는 장군의 과실에서 기인한다. 그 여섯 가지는 도주, 불복종, 와해, 파멸, 혼란, 궤멸이다.

夫勢均, 以一擊十, 曰走.
부 세 균　이 일 격 십　왈 주

Other conditions being equal, if one force is hurled against another ten times its size, the result will be the flight of the former.

피아간의 조건이 동일한 상황에서, 한 부대가 열 배나 큰 부대에게 덤벼들면 작은 부대의 도주가 일어나게 될 것이다.

卒強吏弱, 曰弛.
졸 강 리 약　왈 이

When the common soldiers are too strong and their officers too weak, the result is insubordination.

병사들은 너무 강한데 그들의 장교들은 너무 약하면 불복종이 일어날 것이다.

吏強卒弱, 曰陷.
이 강 졸 약　왈 함

When the officers are too strong and the common soldiers too weak, the result is collapse.

장교들은 너무 강한데 일반 병사들이 너무 약하면 군의 와해가 일어날 것이다.

大吏怒而不服, 遇敵懟而自戰, 將不知其能, 曰崩.
대 리 노 이 불 복　우 적 대 이 자 전　장 부 지 기 능　왈 붕

When the higher officers are angry and insubordinate, and on meeting the enemy give battle on their own account from a feeling of resentment, before the commander-in-chief can tell whether or not he is in a position to fight, the result is ruin.

고급 장교가 화가 나서 상관에게 불복하고, 적과 조우하여 대적할 때 분노로 인해 마음대로 전투를 한다면, 총사령관이 그가 싸울 수 있는 위치에 있는지를 알기도 전에 파멸을 맞이하게 될 것이다.

將弱不嚴, 敎道不明, 吏卒無常 陳兵縱橫, 曰亂.
장 약 불 엄　교 도 불 명　이 졸 무 상　진 병 종 횡　왈 란

When the general is weak and without authority; when his orders are not clear and distinct; when there are no fixed duties assigned to officers and men, and the ranks are formed in a slovenly haphazard manner, the result is utter disorganization.

장군이 나약하고 위엄이 없고, 명령이 명료하고 뚜렷하지 않을 때, 장교와 부하들에게 정해진 임무가 없고 계급이 원칙 없이 멋대로 부여되면, 결과는 완전한 혼란이 될 것이다.

將不能料敵 以少合衆, 以弱擊强 兵無選鋒, 曰北.
장 불 능 료 적　이 소 합 중　이 약 격 강　병 무 선 봉　왈 배

When a general, unable to estimate the enemy's strength, allows an inferior force to engage a larger one, or hurls a weak detachment against a powerful one, and neglects to place picked soldiers in the front rank, the result must be rout.

장군이 적의 전투력을 추정하지 못해 소규모의 아군으로 대규모의 적과 싸우게 하거나 강력한 적에 대항하여 약한 분견대를 투입하고, 선발된 병사를 전방에 배치하는 것을 등한시할 때의 결과는 궤멸이다.

凡此六者, 敗之道也, 將之至任, 不可不察也.
범 차 육 자　패 지 도 야　장 지 지 임　불 가 불 찰 야

These are six ways of courting defeat, which must be carefully noted by the general who has attained a responsible post.

이 여섯 가지는 패배를 자초하는 것들로 책임 있는 직책을 수행하는 장군이 세심하게 유념해야 한다.

夫地形者　兵之助也.　料敵制勝　計險阨遠近
부 지 형 자　병 지 조 야　요 적 제 승　계 험 액 원 근

上將之道也.
상 장 지 도 야

The natural formation of the country is the soldier's best ally; but a power of estimating the adversary, of controlling the forces of victory, and of shrewdly calculating difficulties, dangers and distances, constitutes the test of a great general.

나라의 자연적인 지형은 장병들에게 최고의 협력자이다. 한편 적을 평가하고 승리의 세력을 통제하고 어려움, 위험 요소, 거리 등을 빈틈없이 계산하는 힘은 훌륭한 장군을 평가하는 요소들이다.

知此而用戰者必勝 不知此而用戰者必敗.
지 차 이 용 전 자 필 승   부 지 차 이 용 전 자 필 패

He who knows these things, and in fighting puts his
knowledge into practice, will win his battles. He who
knows them not, nor practices them, will surely be
defeated.

이것을 잘 알고 전투에서 그 지식을 실행으로 옮기면 승리할 것이다. 이것
을 모르고 실천하지도 못하면 반드시 패배한다.

故戰道必勝, 主曰無戰, 必戰可也. 戰道不勝,
고 전 도 필 승   주 왈 무 전   필 전 가 야   전 도 불 승

主曰必戰, 無戰可也.
주 왈 필 전   무 전 가 야

If fighting is sure to result in victory, then you must fight,
even though the ruler forbid it; if fighting will not result
in victory, then you must not fight even at the ruler's
bidding.

전투에서 승리할 것이 확신된다면 군주가 하지 말라고 명령을 하더라도 반
드시 전투를 해야 한다. 전투에서 승리할 수 없음을 안다면 군주가 명령을
해도 전투를 해서는 안 된다.

故進不求名 退不避罪, 惟人是保,
고 진 불 구 명   퇴 불 피 죄   유 인 시 보

而利合於主, 國之寶也.
이 리 합 어 주   국 지 보 야

The general who advances without coveting fame and retreats without fearing disgrace, whose only thought is to protect his country and do good service for his sovereign, is the jewel of the kingdom.

명예를 탐내지 않고 진격하고 불명예를 두려워하지 않고 후퇴하는 장군, 나라를 지키고, 군주를 위하여 훌륭하게 봉사하는 것만을 생각하는 장군은 나라의 보배이다.

視卒如嬰兒, 故可與之赴深溪. 視卒如愛子,
시 졸 여 영 아   고 가 여 지 부 심 계   시 졸 여 애 자

故可與之俱死,
고 가 여 지 구 사

Regard your soldiers as your children, and they will follow you into the deepest valleys; look upon them as your own beloved sons, and they will stand by you even unto death.

병사들을 자기 자식처럼 대하면 가장 깊은 계곡까지도 따를 것이다. 병사들을 사랑하는 아들처럼 보살피면 죽음을 무릅쓰고 곁을 지킬 것이다.

厚而不能使, 愛而不能令, 亂而不能治,
후 이 불 능 사　　애 애 불 능 령　　난 이 불 능 치

譬如驕子, 不可用也.
비 여 교 자　　불 가 용 야

If, however, you are indulgent, but unable to make your authority felt; kind-hearted, but unable to enforce your commands; and incapable, moreover, of quelling disorder: then your soldiers must be likened to spoilt children; they are useless for any practical purpose.

그러나 장군이 병사들에게 너그럽기는 한데 권위를 느끼게 할 수 없고, 인정이 많지만 명령을 따르도록 강제할 수 없고, 게다가 무질서를 평정할 수 없으면 병사들은 버릇없는 애들과 같고 그런 병사들은 실질적인 목적을 위해서는 아무 쓸모가 없다.

知吾卒之可以擊, 而不知敵之不可擊, 勝之半也.
지 오 졸 지 가 이 격　　이 부 지 적 지 불 가 격　　승 지 반 야

If we know that our own men are in a condition to attack, but are unaware that the enemy is not open to attack, we have gone only halfway towards victory.

아군이 적을 공격할 수 있는 조건하에 있다는 것을 알아도 적들이 공격에 무방비하지 않다는 것을 모르면 승리를 향해 반밖에 나아가지 못했을 뿐이다.

知敵之可擊, 而不知吾卒之不可以擊, 勝之半也.
지 적 지 가 격   이 부 지 오 졸 지 불 가 이 격   승 자 반 야

If we know that the enemy is open to attack, but are unaware that our own men are not in a condition to attack, we have gone only halfway towards victory.

적이 공격에 무방비 상태에 있다는 것을 알아도 부하들이 공격할 수 있는 상태가 아니라는 것을 모르면 승리를 향해 반밖에 나아가지 못했을 뿐이다.

知敵之可擊, 知吾卒之可以擊,
지 적 지 가 격   지 오 졸 지 가 이 격

而不知地形之不可以戰, 勝之半也.
이 부 지 지 형 지 불 가 이 전   승 지 반 야

If we know that the enemy is open to attack, and also know that our men are in a condition to attack, but are unaware that the nature of the ground makes fighting impracticable, we have still gone only halfway towards victory.

적이 무방비 상태라는 것을 알고, 아군의 상태가 공격이 가능하다는 것을 알지만 지형 때문에 전투를 하는 것이 현실적으로 불가능하다는 것을 모르면, 아직도 승리를 향해 중간쯤 갔을 뿐이다.

故知兵者, 動而不迷, 擧而不窮.
고 지 병 자　　동 이 불 미　　거 이 불 궁

Hence the experienced soldier, once in motion, is never bewildered; once he has broken camp, he is never at a loss.

그러므로 경험 있는 병사들은 한 번 움직이면 당황하지 않고, 싸우더라도 곤경에 빠지지 않는다.

故曰 : 知彼知己, 勝乃不殆. 知地知天 勝乃可全.
고 왈　　지 피 지 기　　승 내 불 태　　지 지 지 천　승 내 가 전

Hence the saying: If you know the enemy and know yourself, your victory will not stand in doubt; if you know Heaven and know Earth, you may make your victory complete.

그래서 말하기를 적을 알고 나를 알면 우리의 승리는 의심의 여지가 없다. 기상과 지형을 알면 완전한 승리를 할 수 있다.

九地

The Nine Situations

아홉 가지 상황

孫子曰 : 用兵之法, 有散地, 有輕地, 有爭地,
손 자 왈　　　용 병 지 법　　유 산 지　　유 경 지　　유 쟁 지

有交地, 有衢地,
유 교 지　　유 구 지

有重地, 有圮地, 有圍地, 有死地.
유 중 지　　유 비 지　　유 위 지　　유 사 지

Sun Tzu said : The art of war recognizes nine varieties
of ground: (1) Dispersive ground; (2) facile ground; (3)
contentious ground; (4) open ground; (5) ground of
intersecting highways; (6) serious ground; (7) difficult
ground; (8) hemmed-in ground; (9) desperate ground.

손자가 말했다. 병법에서는 지형을 9가지로 분류하여 인식한다. (1) 산지
(散地), (2) 경지(輕地), (3) 쟁지(爭地), (4) 교지(交地), (5) 구지(衢地), (6)
중지(重地), (7) 비지(圮地), (8) 위지(圍地), (9) 사지(死地).

諸侯自戰其地, 爲散地.
제 후 자 전 기 지　　위 산 지

When a chieftain is fighting in his own territory, it is dispersive ground.

제후가 자국의 땅에서 싸울 경우, 이를 산지(散地)라 한다.

入人之地不深者, 爲輕地.
입 인 지 지 불 심 자　　위 경 지

When he has penetrated into hostile territory, but to no great distance, it is facile ground.

적의 영토로 침투하여 들어갔지만 멀리 들어가진 않은 경우 이를 경지(輕地)라 한다.

我得則利, 彼得亦利者, 爲爭地.
아 득 칙 리　　피 득 역 리 자　　위 쟁 지

Ground the possession of which imports great advantage to either side, is contentious ground.

아군이든 적군이든 점령하면 큰 이득을 가져오는 지형을 쟁지(爭地)라 한다.

我可以往, 彼可以來者. 爲交地.
아 가 이 왕   파 가 이 래 자   위 교 지

Ground on which each side has liberty of movement is open ground.

피아 공히 이동의 자유를 가진 지형을 교지(交地)라 한다.

諸侯之地三屬, 先至而得天下衆者, 爲衢地.
제 후 지 지 삼 속   선 지 이 득 천 하 중 자   위 구 지

Ground which forms the key to three contiguous states, so that he who occupies it first has most of the Empire at his command, is a ground of intersecting highways.

인접한 세 나라에게 중요한 지형으로 누구든지 먼저 점령하면 제국의 대부분을 자신의 지휘하에 둘 수 있는 곳이 큰 길이 교차하는 지형인 구지(衢地)이다.

入人之地深, 背城邑多者. 爲重地.
입 인 지 지 심   배 성 읍 다 자   위 중 지

When an army has penetrated into the heart of a hostile country, leaving a number of fortified cities in its rear, it is serious ground.

군대가 적국의 땅에 깊숙이 쳐들어가, 점령한 적의 성읍이 등 뒤에 많이 있는 지역이 중지(重地)이다.

山林險阻沮澤, 凡難行之道者, 爲圮地.
산 림 험 조 저 택　　범 난 행 지 도 자　　위 비 지

Mountain forests, rugged steeps, marshes and fens - all country that is hard to traverse: this is difficult ground.

산림, 바위투성이의 절벽, 늪지와 택지 등 이동하기가 어려운 모든 지역은 힘든 지형, 비지(圮地)이다.

所從由入者隘, 所從歸者迂,
소 종 유 입 자 애　　소 종 귀 자 우

彼寡可以擊我之衆者, 爲圍地.
피 과 가 이 격 아 지 중 자　　위 위 지

Ground which is reached through narrow gorges, and from which we can only retire by tortuous paths, so that a small number of the enemy would suffice to crush a large body of our men: this is hemmed in ground.

협곡을 통해서 닿을 수 있고 구불구불한 길을 통해서만 되돌아 나올 수 있어서 소수의 적으로도 대규모 아군을 부숴버리기에 충분한 '둘러싸인 지형'이 위지(圍地)이다.

疾戰則存, 不疾戰則亡者, 爲死地.
질 전 즉 존　　부 질 전 즉 망 자　　위 사 지

Ground on which we can only be saved from destruction

by fighting without delay, is desperate ground.

지체 없이 싸워서 적을 격파함으로써만 살 수 있는 지형은 사지(死地)다.

是故散地則無戰, 輕地則無止, 爭地則無攻,
시 고 산 지 즉 무 전　　경 지 즉 무 지　　쟁 지 즉 무 공

On dispersive ground, therefore, fight not. On facile ground, halt not. On contentious ground, attack not.

산지에서는 전투를 하지 않는다. 경지에서는 정지하지 않는다. 쟁지에서는 공격하지 않는다.

交地則無絕, 衢地則合交,
교 지 즉 무 절　　구 지 즉 합 교

On open ground, do not try to block the enemy's way. On the ground of intersecting highways, join hands with your allies.

교지에서는 길을 막지 않는다. 구지에서는 동맹국과 손을 잡아라.

重地則掠, 圮地則行,
중 지 즉 략　　비 지 즉 행

On serious ground, gather in plunder. In difficult ground, keep steadily on the march.

중지에서는 약탈하여 물자를 조달한다. 비지에서는 계속하여 행군한다.

圍地則謀, 死地則戰.
위 지 즉 모　　사 지 즉 전

On hemmed-in ground, resort to stratagem. On desperate ground, fight.

위지에서는 책략을 도모하라. 사지에서는 싸워라.

所謂古之善用兵者, 能使敵人, 前後不相及,
소 위 고 지 선 용 병 자　　　능 사 적 인　　　전 후 불 상 급

衆寡不相恃,
중 과 불 상 시

貴賤不相救, 上下不相收,
귀 천 불 상 구　　상 하 불 상 수

Those who were called skillful leaders of old knew how to drive a wedge between the enemy's front and rear; to prevent co-operation between his large and small divisions; to hinder the good troops from rescuing the bad, the officers from rallying their men.

예로부터 숙련된 지도자라 불린 이들은 적군의 전방과 후방이 틀어지게 하고, 대부대와 소부대의 협력을 방해하고, 우수한 부대가 불량한 부대를 구조하지 못하도록 가로막고, 장교들이 부하들을 결집시키지 못하게 한다.

卒離而不集, 兵合而不齊,
졸 이 이 부 집　　병 합 이 부 제

When the enemy's men were united, they managed to
keep them in disorder.

적의 병사들이 단결되어 있으면 그들을 무질서하게 만들었다.

合於利而動, 不合於利而止.
합 어 이 이 동　　불 합 어 리 이 지

When it was to their advantage, they made a forward
move; when otherwise, they stopped still.

유리하면 앞으로 이동하고 그렇지 않으면 정지한다.

敢問, 敵衆整而將來, 待之若何 曰,
감 문　　적 중 정 이 장 래　　대 지 약 하　　왈

先奪其所愛, 則聽矣.
선 탈 기 소 애　　즉 청 의

If asked how to cope with a great host of the enemy in
orderly array and on the point of marching to the attack,
I should say: "Begin by seizing something which your
opponent holds dear; then he will be amenable to your
will."

만약 대열을 정비한 적의 대부대가 공격을 개시하려 할 때 어떻게 대처할 것인가 묻는다면 나는 이렇게 말하겠다. "적이 가장 소중하게 여기는 것을 점령하는 것으로 시작하면 적이 우리의 의도대로 움직일 것이다."

兵之情主速,　乘人之不及,　由不虞之道,
병 지 정 주 속　　승 인 지 불 급　　유 불 우 지 도

攻其所不戒也.
공 기 소 불 계 야

Rapidity is the essence of war: take advantage of the enemy's unreadiness, make your way by unexpected routes, and attack unguarded spots.

전쟁의 요체는 신속함이다. 적의 미비한 상태를 이용하고 예상치 못한 길로 출격하며 경계하지 않는 곳을 공격하라.

凡爲客之道, 深入則專, 主人不克.
범 위 객 지 도　심 입 즉 전　주 인 불 극

The following are the principles to be observed by an invading force: The further you penetrate into a country, the greater will be the solidarity of your troops, and thus the defenders will not prevail against you.

다음은 적국에 침입할 때 준수해야 할 원칙이다. 적국으로 깊이 들어갈수록 부대의 단결력은 더 강력해져서 방어부대는 아군을 당할 수 없을 것이다.

掠於饒野, 三軍足食.
약 어 요 야   삼 군 족 식

Make forays in fertile country in order to supply your
army with food.

부대에 식량을 제공하기 위해서 비옥한 지역으로 진출하라.

謹養而勿勞, 倂氣積力, 運兵計謀, 爲不可測.
근 양 이 물 노   병 기 적 력   운 병 계 모   위 불 가 측

Carefully study the well-being of your men, and do not
overtax them. Concentrate your energy and hoard your
strength. Keep your army continually on the move, and
devise unfathomable plans.

부하들의 복지를 면밀하게 연구하고 지나치게 과세하지 마라. 에너지를 집
중하고 힘을 길러라. 부대를 계속해서 이동시키고 예측할 수 없는 계획을
궁리하라.

投之無所往, 死且不北, 死焉不得, 士人盡力,
투 지 무 소 왕   사 차 불 배   사 언 부 득   사 인 진 력

Throw your soldiers into positions whence there is no
escape, and they will prefer death to flight. If they will
face death, there is nothing they may not achieve. Officers
and men alike will put forth their uttermost strength.

병사들을 빠져나갈 수 없는 곳에 투입하면 도망치기보다는 죽는 쪽을 선택할 것이다. 죽게 될 상황에 직면하면 그들이 못할 것은 아무것도 없다. 장교와 병사들이 똑같이 최고의 전투력을 발휘할 것이다.

兵士甚陷則不懼, 無所往則固, 深入則拘,
병 사 심 함 즉 불 구   무 소 왕 즉 고   심 입 즉 구

不得已則鬪,
부 득 이 즉 투

Soldiers when in desperate straits lose the sense of fear. If there is no place of refuge, they will stand firm. If they are in hostile country, they will show a stubborn front. If there is no help for it, they will fight hard.

최악의 상황에 처한 병사들은 공포감을 상실한다. 도망칠 곳이 없으면 굳세게 버틸 것이다. 그들이 적국에 있을 때에는 완강한 모습을 보여줄 것이다. 도움 받을 길이 없으면 강력하게 싸울 것이다.

是故其兵不修而戒, 不求而得, 不約而親,
시 고 기 병 불 수 이 계   불 구 이 득   불 약 이 친

不令而信,
불 령 이 신

Thus, without waiting to be marshaled, the soldiers will be constantly on the qui vive; without waiting to be asked, they will do your will; without restrictions, they will be faithful; without giving orders, they can be trusted.

그래서 병사들은 통제를 내리지 않아도 스스로 끊임없이 경계하고, 요구를 받지 않아도 장군의 의도를 행할 것이고, 제한하지 않아도 충직할 것이고, 명령하지 않아도 신뢰할 수 있게 된다.

禁祥去疑, 至死無所之.
금 상 거 의   지 사 무 소 지

Prohibit the taking of omens, and do away with superstitious doubts. Then, until death itself comes, no calamity need be feared.

불합리한 징조를 믿거나 미신적인 의심을 하지 않도록 하라. 그러면 죽음이 닥칠 때까지 어떤 재앙도 두려워할 필요가 없다.

吾士無余財, 非惡貨也, 無余命, 非惡壽也.
오 사 무 여 재   비 오 화 야   무 여 명   비 오 수 야

If our soldiers are not overburdened with money, it is not because they have a distaste for riches; if their lives are not unduly long, it is not because they are disinclined to longevity.

아군의 병사들이 돈을 남기지 않는 것은 부를 혐오하기 때문이 아니다. 그들의 목숨이 길지 않은 것은 장수하는 것을 좋아하지 않아서가 아니다.

令發之日, 士卒坐者涕沾襟, 偃臥者涕交頤,
영 발 지 일 사 졸 좌 자 체 점 금   언 와 자 체 교 이

投之無所往者, 諸劌[10]之勇也.
투 지 무 소 왕 자   제 귀 지 용 야

On the day they are ordered out to battle, your soldiers may weep, those sitting up bedewing their garments, and those lying down letting the tears run down their cheeks. But let them once be brought to bay, and they will display the courage of a Chu or a Gui.

전투에 나가라는 명령을 받는 날이면 부하들은 흐느낄 것이다. 앉아 있는 자는 눈물로 옷을 적시고 누워 있는 자는 눈물이 뺨으로 흘러내리리라. 그러나 한번 궁지에 몰리게 되면 그들은 전제와 조귀 못지않은 용맹함을 보일 것이다.

故善用兵者, 譬如率然, 率然者, 常山之蛇也.
고 선 용 병 자   비 여 솔 연   솔 연 자   상 산 지 사 야

The skillful tactician may be likened to the shuai-ran. Now the shuai-jan is a snake that is found in the Chang mountains.

숙련된 전술가는 솔연에 비유할 수 있다. 솔연이란 상산에서 발견되는 뱀이다.

----

10 諸劌는 전제(專諸)와 조귀(曹劌) 두 사람의 이름을 이르는 것으로 전제는 오나라, 조귀는 노나라의 용감한 사람이다.

擊其首則尾至, 擊其尾則首至, 擊其中則首尾俱至.
격 기 수 즉 미 지   격 기 수 즉 수 지   격 기 중 즉 수 미 구 지

Strike at its head, and you will be attacked by its tail; strike at its tail, and you will be attacked by its head; strike at its middle, and you will be attacked by head and tail both.

머리를 치면 꼬리의 공격을 받고, 꼬리를 치면 머리의 공격을 받는다. 가운데를 치면 머리와 꼬리 둘로부터 공격을 받는다.

敢問, 兵可使如率然乎? 曰, 可,
감 문   병 가 사 여 솔 연 호   왈   가

Asked if an army can be made to imitate the shuai-ran, I should answer, Yes.

군대가 솔연을 모방하여 만들어질 수 있는가 묻는다면 나는 그렇다고 할 것이다.

夫吳人與越人相惡也, 當其同舟而濟, 而遇風,
부 오 인 여 월 인 상 오 야   당 기 동 주 이 제   이 우 풍

其相救也, 如左右手.
기 상 구 야   여 좌 우 수

For the men of Wu and the men of Yue are enemies; yet if they are crossing a river in the same boat and are caught by a storm, they will come to each other's assistance just as the left hand helps the right.

오나라와 월나라는 서로 적이지만, 두 나라 사람이 같은 배를 타고 강을 건너다가 폭풍우를 만난다면, 그들은 좌우의 손이 서로 협력하듯 돕게 될 것이다.

是故方馬埋輪, 未足恃也.
시 고 방 마 매 륜   미 족 시 야

Hence it is not enough to put one's trust in the tethering of horses, and the burying of chariot wheels in the ground.

고로 말을 매어두고, 수레바퀴를 파묻어 놓아서 탈주를 막는 것에만 기댈 수는 없다.

齊勇如一, 政之道也. 剛柔皆得, 地之理也.
제 용 여 일   정 지 도 야   강 유 개 득   지 지 리 야

The principle on which to manage an army is to set up one standard of courage which all must reach.

전군을 통제하여 한결같이 용감하게 하나로 일치시켜야 한다.

故善用兵者, 攜手若使一人, 不得已也.
고 선 용 병 자   휴 수 약 사 일 인   부 득 이 야

Thus the skillful general conducts his army just as though he were leading a single man, willy-nilly, by the hand.

그래서 훌륭한 장군은 마치 한 사람의 손을 잡고 이끌듯이 자기 부대를 지휘한다.

將軍之事, 靜以幽, 正以治,
장 군 지 사   정 이 유   정 이 치

It is the business of a general to be quiet and thus ensure secrecy; upright and just, and thus maintain order.

고요하여 비밀을 지키고 고결함과 정의로움을 통해 질서를 유지하는 것이 장군의 본분이다.

能愚士卒之耳目, 使之無知,
능 우 사 졸 지 이 목   사 지 무 지

He must be able to mystify his officers and men by false reports and appearances, and thus keep them in total ignorance.

장군은 거짓 정보와 외양을 통해 장교와 병사들이 계획을 짐작하지 못하고 아무것도 모르게 할 수 있어야 한다.

易其事, 革其謀, 使人無識.
역 기 사　혁 기 모　사 인 무 식

By altering his arrangements and changing his plans, he keeps the enemy without definite knowledge.

부대배치를 변경하고 계획을 바꿈으로써 적들이 확실한 정보를 갖지 못하게 한다.

易其居, 迂其途, 使人不得慮,
역 기 거　우 기 도　사 인 부 득 려

By shifting his camp and taking circuitous routes, he prevents the enemy from anticipating his purpose.

주둔지를 바꾸고 우회로를 택함으로써 적이 아군의 의도를 예측할 수 없게 한다.

帥與之期, 如登高而去其梯,
수 여 지 기　여 등 고 이 거 기 제

At the critical moment, the leader of an army acts like one who has climbed up a height and then kicks away the ladder behind him.

결정적인 시기가 오면 군의 지도자는 높은 곳에 올라간 뒤 뒤에 남겨진 사다리를 차 버리듯이 행동해야 한다.

帥與之深入諸侯之地, 而發其機,
수 여 지 심 입 제 후 지 지   이 발 기 기

He carries his men deep into hostile territory before he shows his hand.

장군은 의도를 알려주기 전에 먼저 부하들을 이끌고 적국 깊숙이 들어간다.

焚舟破釜, 若驅群羊而往, 驅而來, 莫知所之,
분 주 파 부   약 구 군 양 이 왕   구 이 래   막 지 소 지

He burns his boats and breaks his cooking-pots; like a shepherd driving a flock of sheep, he drives his men this way and that, and nothing knows whither he is going.

장군은 배를 불사르고 가마솥을 파괴한다. 마치 목동이 양떼를 몰듯이 부하들을 이리저리 이동시켜서 어디로 가는지를 아무도 알지 못한다.

聚三軍之衆, 投之於險, 此將軍之事也.
취 삼 군 지 중   투 지 어 험   차 장 군 지 사 야

To muster his host and bring it into danger: this may be termed the business of the general.

모든 군사들을 소집하여 위험 속으로 이끌고 가는 것, 이것이 장군의 본분이라고 할 수 있다.

九地之變, 屈伸之利, 人情之理, 不可不察也.
구 지 지 변   굴 신 지 리   인 정 지 리   불 가 불 찰 야

The different measures suited to the nine varieties of
ground; the expediency of aggressive or defensive tactics;
and the fundamental laws of human nature: these are
things that must most certainly be studied.

아홉 가지 다양한 지형에 알맞은 각기 다른 전술, 공격 또는 방어 전술에
따른 방편, 그리고 인간 본성의 근본적인 법칙 등은 가장 철저하게 연구해
야 하는 것들이다.

凡爲客之道, 深則專, 淺則散,
범 위 객 지 도   심 즉 전   천 즉 산

When invading hostile territory, the general principle is,
that penetrating deeply brings cohesion; penetrating but a
short way means dispersion.

적지에 침입했을 때, 일반적으로 깊숙이 침투하면 단결을 불러오지만 단거
리 침투는 분산되어 흩어진다.

去國越境而師者, 絶地也,
거 국 월 경 이 사 자　　절 지 야

When you leave your own country behind, and take your army across neighborhood territory, you find yourself on critical ground.

조국을 뒤로하고 군대와 함께 이웃 영토를 가로지르면 그때는 절지에 있는 것이다.

四達者, 衢地也,
사 달 자　　구 지 야

When there are means of communication on all four sides, the ground is one of intersecting highways.

사방으로 소통할 수단이 있으면 그 지역은 구지이다.

入深者, 重地也, 入淺者, 輕地也.
입 심 자　　중 지 야　　입 천 자　　경 지 야

When you penetrate deeply into a country, it is serious ground. When you penetrate but a little way, it is facile ground.

한 나라 안으로 깊숙이 침투했을 때는 중지에 있다. 짧게 침투할 때는 경지에 있는 것이다.

背固前隘者, 圍地也. 無所往者, 死地也.
배 고 전 애 자　위 지 야　무 소 왕 자　사 지 야

When you have the enemy's strongholds on your rear, and narrow passes in front, it is hemmed-in ground. When there is no place of refuge at all, it is desperate ground.

등 뒤가 적군으로 막히고, 전방이 좁아 협애한 곳이 위지다. 빠져나갈 곳이 전혀 없는 곳에 있으면 사지다.

是故散地, 吾將一其志.
시 고 산 지　오 장 일 기 지

Therefore, on dispersive ground, I would inspire my men with unity of purpose.

그래서 산지에서는 부하들을 격려하여 한마음으로 단결시킨다.

輕地, 吾將使之屬,
경 지　오 장 사 지 속

On facile ground, I would see that there is close connection between all parts of my army.

경지에서는 모든 아군부대가 밀접하게 연결되도록 하고,

爭地, 吾將趨其後,
쟁 지   오 장 추 기 후

On contentious ground, I would hurry up my rear.

쟁지에서는 신속하게 배후를 대비한다.

交地, 吾將謹其守,
교 지   오 장 근 기 수

On open ground, I would keep a vigilant eye on my defenses.

교지에서는 방어를 철저히 한다.

衢地, 吾將固其結,
구 지   오 장 고 기 결

On ground of intersecting highways, I would consolidate my alliances.

구지에서는 동맹을 강화한다.

重地, 吾將繼其食,
중 지   오 장 계 기 식

On serious ground, I would try to ensure a continuous stream of supplies.

중지에서는 지속적인 군수지원이 확실하게 이루어지게 한다.

圮地, 吾將進其途,
비 지　　오 장 진 기 도

On difficult ground, I would keep pushing on along the road.

비지에서는 가던 길을 따라 계속 진격하도록 밀어붙인다.

圍地, 吾將塞其闕,
위 지　　오 장 색 기 궐

On hemmed-in ground, I would block any way of retreat.

위지에서는 퇴로를 막는다.

死地, 吾將示之以不活.
사 지　　오 장 시 지 이 불 활

On desperate ground, I would proclaim to my soldiers the hopelessness of saving their lives.

사지에서는 병사들에게 그들의 생명을 구할 희망이 없음을 선언한다.

故兵之情, 圍則御, 不得已則鬪, 過則從,
고 병 지 정　위 즉 어　부 득 이 즉 투　과 즉 종

For it is the soldier's disposition to offer an obstinate resistance when surrounded, to fight hard when he cannot help himself, and to obey promptly when he has fallen into danger.

병사들은 포위당하면 끝까지 항거하고, 자신을 구할 수 없으면 용감히 전투를 하며, 위험에 처하게 되면 명령에 즉각 복종한다.

是故, 不知諸侯之謀者, 不能預交,
시 고　부 지 제 후 지 모 자　부 능 예 교

We cannot enter into alliance with neighboring princes until we are acquainted with their designs.

주변국의 계획을 잘 알게 되기 전에는 그들 군주와 동맹을 맺을 수 없다.

不知山林, 險阻, 沮澤之形者, 不能行軍,
부 지 산 림　험 조　저 택 지 형 자　불 능 행 군

We are not fit to lead an army on the march unless we are familiar with the face of the country - its mountains and forests, its pitfalls and precipices, its marshes and swamps.

그 나라의 산과 숲, 함정과 절벽, 늪지대 등 지형에 대해서 친숙해지지 않고서는 군대의 행군을 이끄는 것이 불가능하다.

不用鄉導, 不能得地利,
불 용 향 도　불 능 득 지 리

We shall be unable to turn natural advantages to account unless we make use of local guides.

현지의 안내인을 이용하지 않으면 지형의 자연적인 이점을 이용할 수가 없다.

四五者, 不知一, 非霸王之兵也.
사 오 자　부 지 일　비 패 왕 지 병 야

To be ignored of any one of the following four or five principles does not befit a warlike prince.

이 4, 5가지의 원칙 중에서 하나라도 간과하면 전쟁을 잘하는 군주(패왕)라 할 수 없다.

夫霸王之兵, 伐大國, 則其衆不得聚,
부 패 왕 지 병　벌 대 국　즉 기 중 부 득 취

When a warlike prince attacks a powerful state, his generalship shows itself in preventing the concentration of the enemy's forces.

전쟁을 잘하는 군주(패왕)는 강력한 국가를 공격할 때 적군의 단합을 저지하는 것을 통해 장군으로서의 면모를 보여준다.

威加於敵, 則其交不得合.
위 가 어 적   즉 기 교 부 득 합

He overawes his opponents, and their allies are prevented from joining against him.

그는 적을 위압하고 적국의 동맹국들이 아군에 맞서지 못하게 한다.

是故, 不爭天下之交, 不養天下之權,
시 고   부 쟁 천 하 지 교   불 양 천 하 지 권

Hence he does not strive to ally himself with all and sundry, nor does he foster the power of other states.

그러므로 모든 나라들과 동맹을 맺으려 애쓰거나 타국의 세력을 키우는 것을 도우려 하지도 않는다.

信己之私, 威加於敵.
신 기 지 사   위 가 어 적

He carries out his own secret designs, keeping his antagonists in awe.

자신의 비밀스런 계획을 추진하며 적대자들을 두려워하게 만든다.

故其城可拔, 其國可隳也.
고 기 성 가 발   기 국 가 휴 야

Thus he is able to capture their cities and overthrow their kingdoms.

그리하여 적의 성들을 점령하고 그들의 왕국을 전복시킬 수 있다.

施無法之賞, 懸無政之令, 犯三軍之衆, 若使一人.
시 무 법 지 상   현 무 정 지 령   범 삼 군 지 중   약 사 일 인

Bestow rewards without regard to rule, issue orders without regard to previous arrangements; and you will be able to handle a whole army as though you had to do with but a single man.

법에 없는 상을 베풀고, 정사에 없는 명령을 내리라. 그러면 전군을 마치 한 사람처럼 다룰 수 있다.

犯之以事, 勿告以言,
범 지 이 사   물 고 이 언

Confront your soldiers with the deed itself; never let them know your design.

부하들에겐 임무만을 부여하고 계획을 일일이 알려주지 마라.

犯之以利, 勿告以害.
범 지 이 리   물 고 이 해

When the outlook is bright, bring it before their eyes; but
tell them nothing when the situation is gloomy.

전망이 밝을 때는 그 사실을 그들의 눈앞에 보여주어 알게 하고 상황이 불
리할 때는 아무것도 말하지 마라.

投之亡地然後存, 陷之死地然後生,
투 지 망 지 연 후 존   함 지 사 지 연 후 생

Place your army in deadly peril, and it will survive; plunge
it into desperate straits, and it will come off in safety.

군대를 죽음의 위기에 몰아넣으면 군대는 생존할 것이다. 죽음의 계곡에
빠뜨리면 안전하게 벗어날 것이다.

夫衆陷於害, 然後能爲勝敗.
부 중 함 어 해   연 후 능 위 승 패

For it is precisely when a force has fallen into harm's way
that is capable of striking a blow for victory.

병사들은 위급한 상황에 떨어졌을 때 승리의 일격을 가할 수 있게 되기 때
문이다.

故爲兵之事, 在於順祥敵之意,
고 위 병 지 사   재 어 순 상 적 지 의

Success in warfare is gained by carefully accommodating
ourselves to the enemy's purpose.

전쟁에서의 성공은 적이 의도하는 목적에 상응하여 아군을 면밀하게 조정
함으로써 얻어진다.

幷敵一向, 千里殺將,
병 적 일 향   천 리 살 장

By persistently hanging on the enemy's flank, we shall
succeed in the long run in killing the commander-in-chief.

끈질기게 적의 측방을 물고 늘어짐으로써 장기적으로 결국 적장을 살해하
는 데 성공하게 될 것이다.

是謂巧能成事者也.
시 위 교 능 성 사 자 야

This is called ability to accomplish a thing by sheer
cunning.

이런 것을 두고 빛나는 술책으로 목표를 달성하는 능력이라 한다.

是故政擧之日, 夷關折符, 無通其使,
시 고 정 거 지 일　이 관 절 부　무 통 기 사

On the day that you take up your command, block the frontier passes, destroy the official tallies, and stop the passage of all emissaries.

선전포고를 행하는 날은 적국과의 관문을 봉쇄하고 통행증을 폐기하며, 사절의 왕래를 중지하라.

勵於廊廟之上, 以誅其事.
여 어 낭 묘 지 상　이 주 기 사

Be stern in the council-chamber, so that you may control the situation.

회의에서는 강경한 태도를 보여서 상황을 통제하라.

敵人開闔, 必亟入之,
적 인 개 합　필 극 입 지

If the enemy leaves a door open, you must rush in.

적군이 문을 열어두었을 때는 반드시 돌진해 들어간다.

先其所愛, 微與之期,
선 기 소 애   미 여 지 기

Forestall your opponent by seizing what he holds dear, and subtly contrive to time his arrival on the ground.

적이 소중히 여기는 것을 장악함으로써 적의 기선을 제압하고 세밀하게 궁리하여 적이 도달하는 시간을 예측하라.

踐墨隨敵, 以決戰事,
천 묵 수 적   이 결 전 사

Walk in the path defined by rule, and accommodate yourself to the enemy until you can fight a decisive battle.

규정된 행동 방식을 실천하고 결정적인 전투를 할 수 있을 때까지 적이 의도하는 대로 따르는 것처럼 행동하라.

是故始如處女, 敵人開戶, 後如脫, 敵不及拒.
시 고 시 여 처 녀   적 인 개 호   후 여 탈 토   적 불 급 거

At first, then, exhibit the coyness of a maiden, until the enemy gives you an opening; afterwards emulate the rapidity of a running hare, and it will be too late for the enemy to oppose you.

처음에는 적이 틈을 줄 때까지 처녀처럼 수줍은 듯한 모습을 보이고, 그런 후에는 달리는 토끼의 신속함으로 행동하면 적은 아군에게 대응하기에는 이미 늦은 상태가 될 것이다.

火攻

The Attack by Fire
화공

孫子曰 : 凡火攻有五, 一曰火人, 二曰火積,
손 자 왈　　범 화 공 유 오　　일 왈 화 인　　이 왈 화 적

三曰火輜, 四曰火庫, 五曰火隊.
삼 왈 화 치　　사 왈 화 고　　오 왈 화 대

Sun Tzu said : There are five ways of attacking with fire.
The first is to burn soldiers in their camp; the second is to
burn stores; the third is to burn baggage trains; the fourth
is to burn arsenals and magazines; the fifth is to hurl
dropping fire amongst the enemy.

손자가 말했다 : 화공의 방법에는 다섯 가지가 있다. 첫째는 주둔지에 있
는 적병을 불태우는 것이고, 둘째는 군수품 저장 창고를 불태우는 것이고,
셋째는 병참 수송 차량을 불태우는 것이며, 넷째는 무기고와 탄약을 불태
우는 것이고, 다섯째는 적군 가운데에 불을 쏟아붓는 것이다.

行火必有因, 煙火必素具,
행 화 필 유 인　　연 화 필 소 구

In order to carry out an attack, we must have means
available. The material for raising fire should always be

kept in readiness.

화공을 수행하기 위해서는 가용수단을 반드시 확보해야 한다. 불을 피울 재료는 항상 준비된 상태로 있어야 한다.

發火有時, 起火有日,
발 화 유 시　　　기 화 유 일

There is a proper season for making attacks with fire, and special days for starting a conflagration.

불을 놓는 데는 때가 있고 불이 잘 타오르는 날이 있다.

時者, 天之燥也. 日者, 月在, 箕, 壁, 翼, 軫也.
시 자　　천 지 조 야　　일 자　월 재　　기　　벽　　익　　진 야

凡此四宿者, 風起之日也,
범 차 사 숙 자　　풍 기 지 일 야

The proper season is when the weather is very dry; the special days are those when the moon is in the constellations of the Sieve, the Wall, the Wing or the Cross-bar; for these four are all days of rising wind.

적당한 계절이란 날씨가 매우 건조할 때이고, 특별한 날이란 달의 운행이 기(sieve), 벽(wall), 익(wing), 진(cross-over)의 별자리에 존재하는 날이다. 이 네 별자리는 모두 바람이 일어나는 날이다.

凡火攻, 必因五火之變而應之,
범 화 공 필 인 오 화 지 변 이 응 지

In attacking with fire, one should be prepared to meet five possible developments:

화공을 할 때는 다음 다섯 가지 가능한 상황에 대처할 준비가 되어 있어야 한다.

火發於內, 則早應之於外,
화 발 어 내 즉 조 응 지 어 외

(1) When fire breaks out inside to enemy's camp, respond at once with an attack from without.

첫째, 적의 진영에서 불이 났을 때 즉시 적의 외부에서도 공격으로 호응한다.

火發而其兵靜者, 待而勿攻,
화 발 이 기 병 정 자 대 이 물 공

(2) If there is an outbreak of fire, but the enemy's soldiers remain quiet, bide your time and do not attack.

둘째, 불이 났는데도 적의 병사들이 조용히 있으면 아군에게 좋은 시간을 기다리고 공격하지 마라.

極其火力, 可從而從之, 不可從而止,
극 기 화 력 가 종 이 종 지 불 가 종 이 지

(3) When the force of the flames has reached its height,

follow it up with an attack, if that is practicable; if not, stay where you are.

불꽃이 최고조에 이르렀을 때 공격이 가능하면 공격하고 그렇지 않으면 현재 위치에 머물러라.

火可發於外, 無待於內, 以時發之.
화 가 발 어 외　무 대 어 내　이 시 발 지

(4) If it is possible to make an assault with fire from without, do not wait for it to break out within, but deliver your attack at a favorable moment.

셋째, 적진 밖에서 불을 붙이기 편리한 경우에는 적의 내부 상황에 개의치 말고 적당한 때에 불을 지른다.

火發上風, 無攻下風, 晝風久, 夜風止,
화 발 상 풍　무 공 하 풍　주 풍 구　야 풍 지

(5) When you start a fire, be to windward of it. Do not attack from the leeward. A wind that rises in the daytime lasts long, but a night breeze soon falls.

넷째로 불이 바람이 불어오는 쪽에서 일어날 때에는 바람을 받으면서 공격해서는 안 된다. 다섯째로 낮에 일어나는 바람은 오래 불고, 야간에 이는 바람은 곧 잦아든다.

凡軍必知, 有五火之變, 以數守之.
범 군 필 지　　유 오 화 지 변　　이 삭 수 지

In every army, the five developments connected with fire must be known, the movements of the stars calculated, and a watch kept for the proper days.

모든 군대에서는 화공과 관련된 다섯 가지 상황을 반드시 알아야 하며, 별들의 움직임을 잘 계산하고, 적당한 때를 위해 철저히 관찰해야 한다.

故以火佐攻者明, 以水佐攻者强.
고 이 화 좌 공 자 명　　이 수 좌 공 자 강

Hence those who use fire as an aid to the attack show intelligence; those who use water as an aid to the attack gain an accession of strength.

불로써 공격을 돕는 데는 총명한 지혜가 필요하고, 물로써 공격을 돕는 데는 추가적인 힘을 얻는다.

水可以絶, 不可以奪.
수 가 이 절　　불 가 이 탈

By means of water, an enemy may be intercepted, but not robbed of all his belongings.

물을 이용하면 적을 차단할 수 있지만 적의 모든 소유물을 탈취할 수는 없다.

夫戰勝攻取, 而不修其功者凶, 命曰費留.
부 전 승 공 취　　이 불 수 기 공 자 흉　　명 왈 비 류

Unhappy is the fate of one who tries to win his battles and succeed in his attacks without cultivating the spirit of enterprise; for the result is waste of time and general stagnation.

전투에서 애써 승리하고도 그 공적을 기리지 않으면 불운을 맞는다. 결과적으로 시간 낭비가 된 셈이고 전반적인 침체를 불러오기 때문이다.

故曰, 明主慮之, 良將修之.
고 왈　　명 주 려 지　　양 장 수 지

Hence the saying: The enlightened ruler lays his plans well ahead; the good general cultivates his resources.

그래서 말하기를 현명한 군주는 멀리 앞을 내다보고 계획을 수립하고 훌륭한 장군은 그의 자원을 개발한다.

非利不動, 非得不用, 非危不戰.
비 리 부 동　　비 득 불 용　　비 위 부 전

Move not unless you see an advantage; use not your troops unless there is something to be gained; fight not unless the position is critical.

이득이 없으면 전쟁하지 말고, 뭔가 얻을 것이 없으면 부대를 사용하지 말고, 국가가 위기에 있지 않으면 싸우지 마라.

主不可以怒而興師, 將不可以慍而致戰.
주 불 가 이 노 이 흥 사 장 불 가 이 온 이 치 전

No ruler should put troops into the field merely to gratify his own spleen; no general should fight a battle simply out of pique.

어떤 군주도 단지 화를 풀기 위해서 부대를 전쟁터로 보내서는 안 된다. 어떤 장수도 화난다는 이유만으로 전투를 해서는 안 된다.

合於利而動, 不合於利而止.
합 어 리 이 동 불 합 어 리 이 지

If it is to your advantage, make a forward move; if not, stay where you are.

이익에 부합되면 전진하고, 그렇지 않으면 현재 위치에 머물러라.

怒可以復喜, 慍可以復悅,
노 가 이 복 희 온 가 이 복 열

Anger may in time change to gladness; vexation may be succeeded by content.

노여움은 기쁨이 될 수 있고 불편함은 만족으로 변할 수 있다.

亡國不可以復存, 死者不可以復生.
망 국 불 가 이 복 존　　사 자 불 가 이 복 생

But a kingdom that has once been destroyed can never come again into being; nor can the dead ever be brought back to life.

그러나 파괴된 왕국은 다시 존재할 수 없고 죽은 자는 다시 살아날 수 없다.

故明君愼之, 良將警之.
고 명 군 신 지　　양 장 경 지

Hence the enlightened ruler is heedful, and the good general full of caution.

고로 현명한 군주는 신중하고 탁월한 장군은 전쟁을 경계한다.

此安國全軍之道也.
차 안 국 전 군 지 도 야

This is the way to keep a country at peace and an army intact.

이것이 나라를 평화롭게 유지하고 군대를 보존하는 방법이다.

用間

The Use of Spies
간첩의 이용

孫子曰 : 凡興師十萬, 出征千里, 百姓之費,
손 자 왈　　 범 흥 사 십 만　 출 정 천 리　 백 성 지 비

公家之奉, 日費千金.
공 가 지 봉　 일 비 천 금

Sun Tzu said : Raising a host of a hundred thousand men and marching them great distances entails heavy loss on the people and a drain on the resources of the State. The daily expenditure will amount to a thousand ounces of silver.

손자가 말했다: 십만의 군대를 동원하여 원거리를 출정하는 것은 백성들의 큰 손실과 국가 자원의 유출을 초래한다. 일일 지출액이 은 1,000온스에 이를 것이다.

內外騷動, 怠於道路, 不得操事者, 七十萬家,
내 외 소 동　　태 어 도 로　　부 득 조 사 자　　칠 십 만 가

There will be commotion at home and abroad, and men will drop down exhausted on the highways. As many as seven hundred thousand families will be impeded in their labor.

나라의 안팎에 소동이 일어날 것이고, 사람들은 대로에 지쳐 쓰러질 것이다. 70만에 이르는 가구들이 생업에 방해를 받을 것이다.

相守數年, 以爭一日之勝,
상 수 수 년　　이 쟁 일 일 지 승

Hostile armies may face each other for years, striving for the victory which is decided in a single day.

적군을 상대하여 수년간을 대치할 수 있지만, 전쟁의 승패는 하루아침에 결정된다.

而愛爵祿百金, 不知敵之情者, 不仁之至也.
이 애 작 록 백 금　　부 지 적 지 정 자　　불 인 지 지 야

This being so, to remain in ignorance of the enemy's condition simply because one grudges the outlay of a hundred ounces of silver in honors and emoluments, is the height of inhumanity.

이렇다는 건데 단지 간첩에게 보수로 지출할 은 100온스에 인색함으로써 적에 대해 알려고 하지 않는 것은 비인간적인 처사이다.

非人之將也, 非主之佐也, 非勝之主也,
비 인 지 장 야   비 주 지 좌 야   비 승 지 주 야

One who acts thus is no leader of men, no present help to his sovereign, no master of victory.

그렇게 행동하는 자는 부하들의 지도자가 아니며 군주에게 실질적인 도움이 되지 않으며 승리의 주도자도 아니다.

故明君賢將, 所以動而勝人, 成功出於衆者,
고 명 군 현 장   소 이 동 이 승 인   성 공 출 어 중 자

先知也.
선 지 야

Thus, what enables the wise sovereign and the good general to strike and conquer, and achieve things beyond the reach of ordinary men, is foreknowledge.

그러므로 현명한 군주와 탁월한 장군이 공격하여 정복하고 보통 사람들 이상의 출중한 성공을 이루는 이유는 적정을 알기 때문이다.

先知者, 不可取於鬼神, 不可象於事, 不可驗於度,
선 지 자   불 가 취 어 귀 신   불 가 상 어 사   불 가 험 어 도

Now this foreknowledge cannot be elicited from spirits; it cannot be obtained inductively from experience, nor by any deductive calculation.

이는 귀신에게 의지하여 알 수 있거나 경험으로부터 귀납적으로 얻을 수 있는 것도, 연역적 계산으로 얻을 수 있는 것도 아니다.

必取於人, 知敵之情者也.
필 취 어 인   지 적 지 정 자 야

Knowledge of the enemy's dispositions can only be obtained from other men.

적에 대한 지식은 오로지 적을 알고 있는 자로부터만 알 수 있다.

故用間有五, 有鄉間, 有內間, 有反間, 有死間,
고 용 간 유 오   유 향 간   유 내 간   유 반 간   유 사 간

有生間,
유 생 간

Hence the use of spies, of whom there are five classes:

(1) Local spies; (2) inward spies; (3) converted spies; (4) doomed spies; (5) surviving spies.

그러므로 간첩 이용에는 다섯 부류가 있는데, 향간(지역 스파이), 내간(내부 스파이), 반간(전향한 스파이), 사간(배반할 가능성이 있는 첩자에게 거짓 정보를 주어 적의 손에 처형되게 하는 것), 생간(살아 돌아온 스파이)이 있다.

五間俱起, 莫知其道, 是謂神紀, 人君之寶也.
오 간 구 기　막 지 기 도　시 위 신 기　인 군 지 보 야

When these five kinds of spy are all at work, none can discover the secret system. This is called 'divine manipulation of the threads.' It is the sovereign's most precious faculty.

이런 다섯 가지 유형의 간첩이 모두 활동을 하면 누구도 그 비밀 시스템을 알아내지 못한다. 이것은 '신이 내린 솜씨의 실타래'라고 불린다. 이것은 군주의 가장 보배로운 능력이다.

鄕間者, 因其鄕人而用之,
향 간 자　인 기 향 인 이 용 지

Having **local spies** means employing the services of the inhabitants of a district.

향간을 갖는 것은 그 지역의 주민을 고용하는 것을 뜻한다.

內間者, 因其官人而用之,
내 간 자　인 기 관 인 이 용 지

Having **inward spies**, making use of officials of the enemy.

내간을 갖는 것은 적의 관리들을 활용하는 것이다.

反間者, 因其敵間而用之.
반 간 자   인 기 적 간 이 용 지

Having **converted spies**, getting hold of the enemy's spies and using them for our own purposes.

반간을 갖는 것은 적의 간첩을 잡아서 아군의 목적에 맞게 이중간첩으로 사용하는 것이다.

死間者, 爲誑事於外, 令吾聞知之, 而傳於敵間也.
사 간 자   위 광 사 어 외   영 오 문 지 지   이 전 어 적 간 야

Having **doomed spies**, doing certain things openly for purposes of deception, and allowing our spies to know of them and report them to the enemy.

사간을 갖는 것은 사실은 거짓인 정보를 흘려 아군의 간첩(배반할 가능성이 있는 아군 간첩)들이 그것을 적들에게 보고하도록 하는 것이다.

生間者, 反報也.
생 간 자   반 보 야

Surviving spies, finally, are those who bring back news from the enemy's camp.

끝으로 생간은 적진으로부터 소식을 가지고 생환한 아군의 첩자들이다.

故三軍之事, 莫親於間,
고 삼 군 지 사　　막 친 어 간

Hence it is that which none in the whole army are more intimate relations to be maintained than with spies.

그러므로 군대에서 간첩요원과의 관계는 다른 무엇보다도 더 친밀해야 한다.

賞莫厚於間, 事莫密於間,
상 막 후 어 간　　사 막 밀 어 간

None should be more liberally rewarded. In no other business should greater secrecy be preserved.

간첩요원은 더 후하게 포상되어야 한다. 간첩 업무보다 더 철저히 비밀을 유지해야 하는 것은 아무 것도 없다.

非聖智不能用間,
비 성 지 불 능 용 간

Spies cannot be usefully employed without a certain intuitive sagacity.

직관적인 혜안(사람을 알아보는 지혜)이 없으면 간첩을 유용하게 운용할 수 없다.

非仁義不能使間,
비 인 의 불 능 사 간

They cannot be properly managed without benevolence and straightforwardness.

자애로움과 정의심이 없으면 간첩을 적절하게 운용할 수 없다.

非微妙不能得間之實.
비 미 묘 불 능 득 간 지 실

Without subtle ingenuity of mind, one cannot make certain of the truth of their reports.

섬세하고 미묘한 재간이 없으면 간첩요원들의 보고의 진실성을 파악할 수 없다.

微哉微哉, 無所不用間也.
미 재 미 재 무 소 불 용 간 야

Be subtle! be subtle! and use your spies for every kind of business.

교묘하라! 교묘하라! 그리고 첩보요원들을 모든 분야의 일에 활용하라.

間事未發, 而先聞者, 間與所告者皆死.
간 사 미 발　　이 선 문 자　　간 여 소 고 자 개 사

If a secret piece of news is divulged by a spy before the
time is ripe, he must be put to death together with the
man to whom the secret was told.

간첩이 발견되어 미리 알려지면, 간첩은 물론 그 정보를 발설한 자도 모두
죽게 된다.

凡軍之所欲擊, 城之所欲攻, 人之所欲殺,
범 군 지 소 욕 격　　성 지 소 욕 공　　인 지 소 욕 살

必先知其守將,
필 선 지 기 수 장

左右, 謁者, 門者, 舍人之姓名, 令吾間必索知之.
좌 우　　알 자　　문 자　　사 인 지 성 명　　영 오 간 필 색 지 지

Whether the object be to crush an army, to storm a city,
or to assassinate an individual, it is always necessary to
begin by finding out the names of the attendants, the
aides-de-camp, and door-keepers and sentries of the
general in command. Our spies must be commissioned to
ascertain these.

목적이 적을 궤멸시키는 것이든 도시를 습격하는 것이든 개인을 암살하는
것이든 항상 먼저 수행원, 보좌관, 문지기, 사령관, 보초의 이름을 알아내
야 한다. 이러한 것들을 알아내기 위해 아군의 간첩을 임명해야 한다.

必索敵人之間來間我者, 因而利之, 導而舍之,
필 색 적 인 지 간 래 간 아 자　　인 이 리 지　　도 이 사 지

故反間可得而用也.
고 반 간 가 득 이 용 야

The enemy's spies who have come to spy on us must
be sought out, tempted with bribes, led away and
comfortably housed. Thus they will become converted
spies and available for our service.

아군의 정보를 수집하려고 들어온 적국의 간첩을 필히 수색하여 찾아내고,
뇌물로 포섭하고, 유인하여 안락한 집을 제공해야 한다. 그렇게 하면 그들
은 반간이 되어 우리에게 필요한 일을 할 수 있게 될 것이다.

因是而知之, 故鄕間, 內間可得而使也.
인 시 이 지 지　　고 향 간　　내 간 가 득 이 사 야

It is through the information brought by the converted
spy that we are able to acquire and employ local and
inward spies.

반간으로부터 가져온 정보를 통하여 향간과 내간을 확보하여 운용할 수 있다.

因是而知之. 故死間爲誑事可使告敵,
인 시 이 지 지　　고 사 간 위 광 사 가 사 고 적

It is owing to his information, again, that we can cause the doomed spy to carry false tidings to the enemy.

또한 반간의 정보에 의해서 아군은 사간이 적군에게 잘못된 정보를 전달하게 할 수 있다.

因是而知之, 故生間, 可使如期.
인 시 이 지 지　　고 생 간　　가 사 여 기

Lastly, it is by his information that the surviving spy can be used on appointed occasions.

마지막으로 그의 정보를 통해서 생간이 특정 상황에 맞게 사용될 수 있다.

五間之事, 君必知之, 知之必在於反間,
오 간 지 사　　군 필 지 지　　지 지 필 재 어 반 간

The end and aim of spying in all its five varieties is knowledge of the enemy; and this knowledge can only be derived, in the first instance, from the converted spy.

이 다섯 가지 간첩 운용의 목적은 적에 대한 정보이고, 이 정보는 우선 먼저 반간으로부터 얻을 수 있다.

故反間不可不厚也.
고 반 간 불 가 불 후 야

Hence it is essential that the converted spy be treated with
the utmost liberality.

그러므로 반간은 반드시 최고의 관대함으로 대우해야 한다.

昔殷之興也, 伊摯在夏,
석 은 지 흥 야   이 지 재 하

Of old, the rise of the Yin dynasty was due to Yi Zhi
who had served under the Xia.

옛날에, 은 왕조는 하나라에서 일했던 이지 덕분에 부흥할 수 있었다.

周之興也. 呂牙在殷.
주 지 흥 야   여 아 재 은

Likewise, the rise of the Zhou dynasty was due to Lu Ya
who had served under the Yin.

마찬가지로 주 왕조의 부흥은 은나라에서 일했던 여아가 있었기 때문이다.

故惟明君賢將, 能以上智爲間者, 必成大功,
고 유 명 군 현 장　능 이 상 지 위 간 자　필 성 대 공

Hence it is only the enlightened ruler and the wise general who will use the highest intelligence of the army for purposes of spying and thereby they achieve great results.

그러므로 명석한 군주와 현명한 장군만이 뛰어난 지혜를 가지고 간첩을 사용하여 위대한 결과를 성취한다.

此兵之要, 三軍之所恃而動也.
차 병 지 요　삼 군 지 소 시 이 동 야

Spies are a most important element in war, because on them depends an army's ability to move.

간첩은 전쟁에서 가장 중요한 요소의 하나다. 전군이 그 활동을 믿고 기동하게 되는 것이다.

부

록

Sun Tzu

THE ART
OF WAR

Lionel Giles

CONTENTS

Chapter 1

Laying Plans

Sun Tzu said: The art of war is of vital importance to the State.

It is a matter of life and death, a road either to safety or to ruin. Hence it is a subject of inquiry which can on no account be neglected.

The art of war, then, is governed by five constant factors, to be taken into account in one' s deliberations, when seeking to determine the conditions obtaining in the field.

These are: (1) The Moral Law; (2) Heaven; (3) Earth; (4) The Commander; (5) Method and discipline.

The Moral Law causes the people to be in

complete accord with their ruler, so that they will follow him regardless of their lives, undismayed by any danger.

Heaven signifies night and day, cold and heat, times and seasons.

Earth comprises distances, great and small; danger and security; open ground and narrow passes; the chances of life and death.

The Commander stands for the virtues of wisdom, sincerity, benevolence, courage and strictness.

By method and discipline are to be understood the marshaling of the army in its proper subdivisions, the graduations of rank among the officers, the maintenance of roads by which supplies may reach the army, and the control of military expenditure.

These five heads should be familiar to every general: he who knows them will be victorious; he who knows them not will fail.

Therefore, in your deliberations, when seeking

to determine the military conditions, let them be made the basis of a comparison, in this wise:—

(1) Which of the two sovereigns is imbued with the Moral Law?
(2) Which of the two generals has most ability?
(3) With whom lie the advantages derived from Heaven and Earth?
(4) On which side is discipline most rigorously enforced?
(5) Which army is stronger?
(6) On which side are officers and men more highly trained?
(7) In which army is there the greater constancy both in reward and punishment?

By means of these seven considerations I can forecast victory or defeat.

The general that hearkens to my counsel and acts upon it, will conquer: let such a one be retained in command!

The general that hearkens not to my counsel nor acts upon it, will suffer defeat:—let such a one be dismissed!

While heeding the profit of my counsel, avail yourself also of any helpful circumstances over and beyond the ordinary rules.

According as circumstances are favorable, one should modify one's plans.

All warfare is based on deception.

Hence, when able to attack, we must seem unable; when using our forces, we must seem inactive; when we are near, we must make the enemy believe we are far away; when far away, we must make him believe we are near.

Hold out baits to entice the enemy. Feign disorder, and crush him.

If he is secure at all points, be prepared for him. If he is in superior strength, evade him.

If your opponent is of choleric temper, seek to irritate him. Pretend to be weak, that he may grow

The Art of War

arrogant.

If he is taking his ease, give him no rest. If his forces are united, separate them.

Attack him where he is unprepared, appear where you are not expected.

These military devices, leading to victory, must not be divulged beforehand.

Now the general who wins a battle makes many calculations in his temple ere the battle is fought. The general who loses a battle makes but few calculations beforehand.

Thus do many calculations lead to victory, and few calculations to defeat: how much more no calculation at all! It is by attention to this point that I can foresee who is likely to win or lose.

Chapter 2

Waging War

Sun Tzu said: In the operations of war, where there are in the field a thousand swift chariots, as many heavy chariots, and a hundred thousand mail-clad soldiers, with provisions enough to carry them a thousand li, the expenditure at home and at the front, including entertainment of guests, small items such as glue and paint, and sums spent on chariots and armor, will reach the total of a thousand ounces of silver per day. Such is the cost of raising an army of 100,000 men.

When you engage in actual fighting, if victory is long in coming, then men's weapons will grow dull and their ardor will be damped.

If you lay siege to a town, you will exhaust your strength.

Again, if the campaign is protracted, the resources of the State will not be equal to the strain.

Now, when your weapons are dulled, your ardor damped, your strength exhausted and your treasure spent, other chieftains will spring up to take advantage of your extremity.

Then no man, however wise, will be able to avert the consequences that must ensue.

Thus, though we have heard of stupid haste in war, cleverness has never been seen associated with long delays.

There is no instance of a country having benefited from prolonged warfare.

It is only one who is thoroughly acquainted with the evils of war that can thoroughly understand the profitable way of carrying it on.

The skillful soldier does not raise a second levy, neither are his supply-wagons loaded more than twice.

Bring war material with you from home, but forage on the enemy.

Thus the army will have food enough for its needs.

Poverty of the State exchequer causes an army to be maintained by contributions from a distance.

Contributing to maintain an army at a distance causes the people to be impoverished.

On the other hand, the proximity of an army causes prices to go up; and high prices cause the people's substance to be drained away.

When their substance is drained away, the peasantry will be afflicted by heavy exactions.

With this loss of substance and exhaustion of strength, the homes of the people will be stripped bare, and three-tenths of their income will be dissipated; while government expenses for broken chariots, wornout horses, breast-plates and helmets, bows and arrows, spears and shields, protective mantles, draught-oxen and heavy wagons, will amount to four-tenths of its total revenue.

Hence a wise general makes a point of foraging on the enemy.

One cartload of the enemy's provisions is equivalent to twenty of one's own, and likewise a single picul of his provender is equivalent to twenty from one's own store.

Now in order to kill the enemy, our men must be roused to anger; that there may be advantage from defeating the enemy, they must have their rewards.

Therefore in chariot fighting, when ten or more chariots have been taken, those should be rewarded who took the first.

Our own flags should be substituted for those of the enemy, and the chariots mingled and used in conjunction with ours.

The captured soldiers should be kindly treated and kept.

This is called, using the conquered foe to augment one's own strength.

In war, then, let your great object be victory, not lengthy campaigns.

Thus it may be known that the leader of armies is the arbiter of the people's fate, the man on whom it depends whether the nation shall be in peace or in peril.

Chapter 3

Attack by Stratagem

Sun Tzu said : In the practical art of war, the best thing of all is to take the enemy's country whole and intact; to shatter and destroy it is not so good. So, too, it is better to recapture an army entire than to destroy it, to capture a regiment, a detachment or a company entire than to destroy them.

Hence to fight and conquer in all your battles is not supreme excellence; supreme excellence consists in breaking the enemy's resistance without fighting.

Thus the highest form of generalship is to balk the enemy's plans; the next best is to prevent the junction of the enemy's forces; the next in order is to attack the enemy's army in the field; and the worst policy of all is to besiege walled cities.

The rule is, not to besiege walled cities if it can possibly be avoided.

The preparation of mantlets, movable shelters, and various implements of war, will take up three whole months; and the piling up of mounds over against the walls will take three months more.

The general, unable to control his irritation, will launch his men to the assault like swarming ants, with the result that one-third of his men are slain, while the town still remains untaken. Such are the disastrous effects of a siege.

Therefore the skillful leader subdues the enemy's troops without any fighting; he captures their cities without laying siege to them; he overthrows their kingdom without lengthy operations in the field.

With his forces intact he will dispute the mastery of the Empire, and thus, without losing a man, his triumph will be complete. This is the method of attacking by stratagem.

It is the rule in war, if our forces are ten to the enemy's one, to surround him; if five to one, to attack him; if twice as numerous, to divide our army into two.

If equally matched, we can offer battle; if slightly inferior in numbers, we can avoid the enemy; if quite unequal in every way, we can flee from him. Hence, though an obstinate fight may be made by a small force, in the end it must be captured by the larger force.

Now the general is the bulwark of the State; if the bulwark is complete at all points; the State will be strong; if the bulwark is defective, the State will be weak.

There are three ways in which a ruler can bring

misfortune upon his army:

(1) By commanding the army to advance, being ignorant of the fact that it cannot advance; or commanding the army to retreat, being ignorant of the fact that it cannot retreat. This is called hobbling the army.

(2) By attempting to govern an army in the same way as he administers a kingdom, being ignorant of the conditions which obtain in an army. This causes restlessness in the soldier's minds.

(3) By employing the officers of his army without discrimination, through ignorance of the military principle of adaptation to circumstances. This shakes the confidence of the soldiers.

But when the army is restless and distrustful, trouble is sure to come from the other feudal princes. This is simply bringing anarchy into the army, and flinging victory away.

Thus we may know that there are five essentials

for victory:

He will win who knows when to fight and when not to fight.

He will win who knows how to handle both superior and inferior forces.

He will win whose army is animated by the same spirit throughout all its ranks.

He will win who, prepared himself, waits to take the enemy unprepared.

He will win who has military capacity and is not interfered with by the sovereign.

These five are the way by which we know which side will win.

Hence the saying: If you know the enemy and know yourself, you need not fear the result of a hundred battles.

If you know yourself but not the enemy, for every victory gained you will also suffer a defeat.

If you know neither the enemy nor yourself, you will succumb in every battle.

Chapter 4

Tactical Disposition

Sun Tzu said : The good fighters of old first put themselves beyond the possibility of defeat, and then waited for an opportunity of defeating the enemy.

To secure ourselves against defeat lies in our own hands, but the opportunity of defeating the enemy is provided by the enemy himself.

Thus the good fighter is able to secure himself against defeat, but cannot make certain of defeating the enemy.

Hence the saying: One may know how to conquer without being able to do it.

Security against defeat implies defensive tactics; ability to defeat the enemy means taking the offensive.

Standing on the defensive indicates insufficient strength; attacking, a superabundance of strength. The general who is skilled in defense hides in the most secret recesses of the earth; he who is skilled in attack flashes forth from the topmost heights of heaven.

Thus on the one hand we have ability to protect ourselves; on the other, a victory that is complete.

To see victory only when it is within the ken of the common herd is not the acme of excellence.

Neither is it the acme of excellence if you fight and conquer and the whole Empire says, "Well done!"

To lift an autumn hair is no sign of great strength; to see the sun and moon is no sign of sharp sight; to hear the noise of thunder is no sign of a quick ear.

What the ancients called a clever fighter is one who not only wins, but excels in winning with ease.

Hence his victories bring him neither reputation

for wisdom nor credit for courage. He wins his battles by making no mistakes.

Making no mistakes is what establishes the certainty of victory, for it means conquering an enemy that is already defeated.

Hence the skillful fighter puts himself into a position which makes defeat impossible, and does not miss the moment for defeating the enemy.

Thus it is that in war the victorious strategist only seeks battle after the victory has been won, whereas he who is destined to defeat first fights and afterwards looks for victory.

The consummate leader cultivates the moral law, and strictly adheres to method and discipline; thus it is in his power to control success.

In respect of military method, we have, firstly, Measurement; secondly, Estimation of quantity; thirdly, Calculation; fourthly, Balancing of chances; fifthly, Victory.

Measurement owes its existence to Earth; Estimation of quantity to Measurement;

Calculation to Estimation of quantity; Balancing of chances to Calculation; and Victory to Balancing of chances.

A victorious army opposed to a routed one, is as a pound's weight placed in the scale against a single grain. A defeated army is like a gram compared to a pound.

The onrush of a conquering force is like the bursting of pent-up waters into a chasm a thousand fathoms deep.

Chapter 5

Energy

Sun Tzu said : The control of a large force is the same principle as the control of a few men: it is merely a question of dividing up their numbers. Fighting with a large army under your command is nowise different from fighting with a small one: it is merely a question of instituting signs and signals.

To ensure that your whole host may withstand the brunt of the enemy's attack and remain unshaken - this is effected by maneuvers direct and indirect. That the impact of your army may be like a grindstone dashed against an egg - this is effected by the science of weak points and strong.

In all fighting, the direct method may be used for joining battle, but indirect methods will be needed in order to secure victory.

Indirect tactics, efficiently applied, are inexhaustible as Heaven and Earth, unending as the flow of rivers and streams; like the sun and moon, they end but to begin anew; like the four seasons, they pass away to return once more.

There are not more than five musical notes, yet the combinations of these five give rise to more melodies than can ever be heard.

There are not more than five primary colors (blue, yellow, red, white, and black), yet in combination they produce more hues than can ever been seen.

There are not more than five cardinal tastes (sour, acrid, salt, sweet, bitter), yet combinations of them yield more flavors than can ever be tasted.

In battle, there are not more than two methods of attack - the direct and the indirect; yet these two in combination give rise to an endless series of maneuvers.

The direct and the indirect lead on to each other in

turn. It is like moving in a circle - you never come to an end. Who can exhaust the possibilities of their combination?

The onset of troops is like the rush of a torrent which will even roll stones along in its course.

The quality of decision is like the well-timed swoop of a falcon which enables it to strike and destroy its victim.

Therefore the good fighter will be terrible in his onset, and prompt in his decision.

Energy may be likened to the bending of a crossbow; decision, to the releasing of a trigger.

Amid the turmoil and tumult of battle, there may be seeming disorder and yet no real disorder at all; amid confusion and chaos, your array may be without head or tail, yet it will be proof against defeat.

Simulated disorder postulates perfect discipline, simulated fear postulates courage; simulated weakness postulates strength.

Hiding order beneath the cloak of disorder is simply a question of subdivision; concealing courage under a show of timidity presupposes a fund of latent energy; masking strength with weakness is to be effected by tactical dispositions.

Thus one who is skillful at keeping the enemy on the move maintains deceitful appearances, according to which the enemy will act.

He sacrifices something, that the enemy may snatch at it.

By holding out baits, he keeps him on the march; then with a body of picked men he lies in wait for him.

The clever combatant looks to the effect of combined energy, and does not require too much from individuals. Hence his ability to pick out the right men and utilize combined energy.

When he utilizes combined energy, his fighting men become as it were like unto rolling logs or stones.

For it is the nature of a log or stone to remain motionless on level ground, and to move when on a slope; if four-cornered, to come to a standstill, but if round-shaped, to go rolling down.

Thus the energy developed by good fighting men is as the momentum of a round stone rolled down a mountain thousands of feet in height. So much on the subject of energy.

chapter 6

Weak Points and Strong

Sun Tzu said : Whoever is first in the field and awaits the coming of the enemy, will be fresh for the fight; whoever is second in the field and has to hasten to battle will arrive exhausted.

Therefore the clever combatant imposes his will on the enemy, but does not allow the enemy's will to be imposed on him.

By holding out advantages to him, he can cause the enemy to approach of his own accord; or, by inflicting damage, he can make it impossible for the enemy to draw near.

If the enemy is taking his ease, he can harass him; if well supplied with food, he can starve him out;

if quietly encamped, he can force him to move.

Appear at points which the enemy must hasten to defend; march swiftly to places where you are not expected.

An army may march great distances without distress, if it marches through country where the enemy is not.

You can be sure of succeeding in your attacks if you only attack places which are undefended.

You can ensure the safety of your defense if you only hold positions that cannot be attacked.

Hence that general is skillful in attack whose opponent does not know what to defend; and he is skillful in defense whose opponent does not know what to attack.

O divine art of subtlety and secrecy! Through you we learn to be invisible, through you inaudible; and hence we can hold the enemy's fate in our hands.

You may advance and be absolutely irresistible, if you make for the enemy's weak points; you may retire and be safe from pursuit if your movements are more rapid than those of the enemy.

If we wish to fight, the enemy can be forced to an engagement even though he be sheltered behind a high rampart and a deep ditch.

All we need to do is attack some other place that he will be obliged to relieve.

If we do not wish to fight, we can prevent the enemy from engaging us even though the lines of our encampment be merely traced out on the ground.

By discovering the enemy's dispositions and remaining invisible ourselves, we can keep our forces concentrated, while the enemy's must be divided.

We can form a single united body, while the enemy must split up into fractions.

Hence there will be a whole pitted against separate parts of a whole, which means that we shall be many to the enemy's few.

And if we are able thus to attack an inferior force

with a superior one, our opponents will be in dire straits.

The spot where we intend to fight must not be made known; for then the enemy will have to prepare against a possible attack at several different points; and his forces being thus distributed in many directions, the numbers we shall have to face at any given point will be proportionately few.

For should the enemy strengthen his van, he will weaken his rear; should he strengthen his rear, he will weaken his van; should he strengthen his left, he will weaken his right; should he strengthen his right, he will weaken his left.
If he sends reinforcements everywhere, he will everywhere be weak.

Numerical weakness comes from having to prepare against possible attacks; numerical strength, from compelling our adversary to make these preparations against us.

The Art of War

Knowing the place and the time of the coming battle, we may concentrate from the greatest distances in order to fight.

But if neither time nor place be known, then the left wing will be impotent to succor the right, the right equally impotent to succor the left, the van unable to relieve the rear, or the rear to support the van.

How much more so if the furthest portions of the army are anything under a hundred li apart, and even the nearest are separated by several li!

Though according to my estimate the soldiers of Yue exceed our own in number, that shall advantage them nothing in the matter of victory.

I say then that victory can be achieved. Though the enemy be stronger in numbers, we may prevent him from fighting.

Scheme so as to discover his plans and the likelihood of their success.

Rouse him, and learn the principle of his activity

or inactivity.

Force him to reveal himself, so as to find out his vulnerable spots.

Carefully compare the opposing army with your own, so that you may know where strength is superabundant and where it is deficient.

In making tactical dispositions, the highest pitch you can attain is to conceal them; conceal your dispositions, and you will be safe from the prying of the subtlest spies, from the machinations of the wisest brains.

How victory may be produced for them out of the enemy's own tactics - that is what the multitude cannot comprehend.

All men can see the tactics whereby I conquer, but what none can see is the strategy out of which victory is evolved.

Do not repeat the tactics which have gained you one victory, but let your methods be regulated by the infinite variety of circumstances.

Military tactics are like unto water; for water in

its natural course runs away from high places and hastens downwards.

So in war, the way is to avoid what is strong and to strike at what is weak.

Water shapes its course according to the nature of the ground over which it flows; the soldier works out his victory in relation to the foe whom he is facing.

Therefore, just as water retains no constant shape, so in warfare there are no constant conditions.

He who can modify his tactics in relation to his opponent and thereby succeed in winning, may be called a heaven-born captain.

The five elements (water, fire, wood, metal, earth) are not always equally predominant; the four seasons make way for each other in turn.

There are short days and long; the moon has its periods of waning and waxing.

chapter 7

Maneuvering

Sun Tzu said : In war, the general receives his commands from the sovereign.

Having collected an army and concentrated his forces, he must blend and harmonize the different elements thereof before pitching his camp.

After that, comes tactical maneuvering, than which there is nothing more difficult.

The difficulty of tactical maneuvering consists in turning the devious into the direct, and misfortune into gain.

Thus, to take a long and circuitous route, after enticing the enemy out of the way, and though starting after him, to contrive to reach the goal before him, shows knowledge of the artifice of deviation.

Maneuvering with an army is advantageous; with an undisciplined multitude, most dangerous.

If you set a fully equipped army in march in order to snatch an advantage, the chances are that you will be too late.

On the other hand, to detach a flying column for the purpose involves the sacrifice of its baggage and stores.

Thus, if you order your men to roll up their buff-coats, and make forced marches without halting day or night, covering double the usual distance at a stretch, doing a hundred li in order to wrest an advantage, the leaders of all your three divisions will fall into the hands of the enemy.

The stronger men will be in front, the jaded ones will fall behind, and on this plan only one-tenth of your army will reach its destination.

If you march fifty li in order to outmaneuver

the enemy, you will lose the leader of your first division, and only half your force will reach the goal.

If you march thirty li with the same object, two-thirds of your army will arrive.

We may take it then that an army without its baggage-train is lost; without provisions it is lost; without bases of supply it is lost.

We cannot enter into alliances until we are acquainted with the designs of our neighbors.

We are not fit to lead an army on the march unless we are familiar with the face of the country - its mountains and forests, its pitfalls and precipices, its marshes and swamps.

We shall be unable to turn natural advantage to account unless we make use of local guides.

In war, practice dissimulation, and you will succeed.

Whether to concentrate or to divide your troops, must be decided by circumstances.

Let your rapidity be that of the wind, your compactness that of the forest.

In raiding and plundering be like fire, is immovability like a mountain.

Let your plans be dark and impenetrable as night, and when you move, fall like a thunderbolt.

When you plunder a countryside, let the spoil be divided amongst your men; when you capture new territory, cut it up into allotments for the benefit of the soldiery.

Ponder and deliberate before you make a move. He will conquer who has learnt the artifice of deviation. Such is the art of maneuvering.

The Book of Army Management says: On the field of battle, the spoken word does not carry far enough: hence the institution of gongs and drums. Nor can ordinary objects be seen clearly enough: hence the institution of banners and flags.

Gongs and drums, banners and flags, are means whereby the ears and eyes of the host may be focused on one particular point.

The host thus forming a single united body, is it impossible either for the brave to advance alone, or for the cowardly to retreat alone. This is the art of handling large masses of men.

In night-fighting, then, make much use of signal-fires and drums, and in fighting by day, of flags and banners, as a means of influencing the ears and eyes of your army.

A whole army may be robbed of its spirit; a commander-in-chief may be robbed of his presence of mind.

Now a soldier's spirit is keenest in the morning; by noonday it has begun to flag; and in the evening, his mind is bent only on returning to camp.

A clever general, therefore, avoids an army when its spirit is keen, but attacks it when it is sluggish and inclined to return. This is the art of studying moods.

Disciplined and calm, to await the appearance of disorder and hubbub amongst the enemy - this is the art of retaining self-possession.

To be near the goal while the enemy is still far from it, to wait at ease while the enemy is toiling and struggling, to be well-fed while the enemy is famished - this is the art of husbanding one's strength.

To refrain from intercepting an enemy whose banners are in perfect order, to refrain from attacking an army drawn up in calm and confident array - this is the art of studying circumstances.

It is a military axiom not to advance uphill against the enemy, nor to oppose him when he comes downhill.

Do not pursue an enemy who simulates flight; do not attack soldiers whose temper is keen.

Do not swallow bait offered by the enemy. Do not interfere with an army that is returning home.

When you surround an army, leave an outlet free. Do not press a desperate foe too hard. Such is the art of warfare.

chapter 8

Variation in Tactics

Sun Tzu said : In war, the general receives his
commands from the sovereign, collects his army
and concentrates his forces.

roads intersect, join hands with your allies. Do
not linger in dangerously isolated positions.
In hemmed-in situations, you must resort to
stratagem. In desperate position, you must fight.

There are roads which must not be followed,
armies which must be not attacked, towns which
must be besieged, positions which must not be
contested, commands of the sovereign which must
not be obeyed.

The general who thoroughly understands the
advantages that accompany variation of tactics

knows how to handle his troops.

The general who does not understand these, may be well acquainted with the configuration of the country, yet he will not be able to turn his knowledge to practical account.

So, the student of war who is unversed in the art of war of varying his plans, even though he be acquainted with the Five Advantages, will fail to make the best use of his men.

Hence in the wise leader's plans, considerations of advantage and of disadvantage will be blended together.

If our expectation of advantage be tempered in this way, we may succeed in accomplishing the essential part of our schemes.

If, on the other hand, in the midst of difficulties we are always ready to seize an advantage, we may extricate ourselves from misfortune.

Reduce the hostile chiefs by inflicting damage on them; and make trouble for them, and keep them constantly engaged; hold out specious allurements, and make them rush to any given point.

The art of war teaches us to rely not on the likelihood of the enemy's not coming, but on our own readiness to receive him; not on the chance of his not attacking, but rather on the fact that we have made our position unassailable.

There are five dangerous faults which may affect a general:

(1) Recklessness, which leads to destruction;

(2) cowardice, which leads to capture;

(3) a hasty temper, which can be provoked by insults;

(4) a delicacy of honor which is sensitive to shame;

(5) over-solicitude for his men, which exposes him to worry and trouble.

These are the five besetting sins of a general, ruinous to the conduct of war.

When an army is overthrown and its leader slain, the cause will surely be found among these five dangerous faults. Let them be a subject of meditation.

chapter 9

The Army on the March

Sun Tzu said : We come now to the question of encamping the army, and observing signs of the enemy. Pass quickly over mountains, and keep in the neighborhood of valleys.

Camp in high places, facing the sun. Do not climb heights in order to fight. So much for mountain warfare.

After crossing a river, you should get far away from it.

When an invading force crosses a river in its onward march, do not advance to meet it in mid-stream. It will be best to let half the army get across, and then deliver your attack.

If you are anxious to fight, you should not go

to meet the invader near a river which he has to cross.

Moor your craft higher up than the enemy, and facing the sun. Do not move up-stream to meet the enemy. So much for river warfare.

In crossing salt-marshes, your sole concern should be to get over them quickly, without any delay.

If forced to fight in a salt-marsh, you should have water and grass near you, and get your back to a clump of trees. So much for operations in salt-marches.

In dry, level country, take up an easily accessible position with rising ground to your right and on your rear, so that the danger may be in front, and safety lie behind. So much for campaigning in flat country.

These are the four useful branches of military knowledge which enabled the Yellow Emperor to vanquish four several sovereigns.

All armies prefer high ground to low and sunny places to dark.

The Art of War

If you are careful of your men, and camp on hard ground, the army will be free from disease of every kind, and this will spell victory.

When you come to a hill or a bank, occupy the sunny side, with the slope on your right rear. Thus you will at once act for the benefit of your soldiers and utilize the natural advantages of the ground.

When, in consequence of heavy rains up-country, a river which you wish to ford is swollen and flecked with foam, you must wait until it subsides. Country in which there are precipitous cliffs with torrents running between, deep natural hollows, confined places, tangled thickets, quagmires and crevasses, should be left with all possible speed and not approached.

While we keep away from such places, we should get the enemy to approach them; while we face them, we should let the enemy have them on his rear.

If in the neighborhood of your camp there should be any hilly country, ponds surrounded by aquatic grass, hollow basins filled with reeds, or woods with thick undergrowth, they must be carefully routed out and searched; for these are places where men in ambush or insidious spies are likely to be lurking.

When the enemy is close at hand and remains quiet, he is relying on the natural strength of his position.

When he keeps aloof and tries to provoke a battle, he is anxious for the other side to advance.

If his place of encampment is easy of access, he is tendering a bait.

Movement amongst the trees of a forest shows that the enemy is advancing.

The appearance of a number of screens in the midst of thick grass means that the enemy wants to make us suspicious.

The rising of birds in their flight is the sign of an

ambuscade. Startled beasts indicate that a sudden attack is coming.

When there is dust rising in a high column, it is the sign of chariots advancing; when the dust is low, but spread over a wide area, it betokens the approach of infantry.

When it branches out in different directions, it shows that parties have been sent to collect firewood.

A few clouds of dust moving to and fro signify that the army is encamping.

Humble words and increased preparations are signs that the enemy is about to advance.

Violent language and driving forward as if to the attack are signs that he will retreat.

When the light chariots come out first and take up a position on the wings, it is a sign that the enemy is forming for battle.

Peace proposals unaccompanied by a sworn covenant indicate a plot.

When there is much running about and the soldiers fall into rank, it means that the critical moment has come.

When some are seen advancing and some retreating, it is a lure.

When the soldiers stand leaning on their spears, they are faint from want of food.

If those who are sent to draw water begin by drinking themselves, the army is suffering from thirst.

If the enemy sees an advantage to be gained and makes no effort to secure it, the soldiers are exhausted.

If birds gather on any spot, it is unoccupied.

Clamor by night betokens nervousness.

If there is disturbance in the camp, the general's authority is weak.

If the banners and flags are shifted about, sedition is afoot.

If the officers are angry, it means that the men are weary.

When an army feeds its horses with grain and kills its cattle for food, and when the men do not hang their cooking-pots over the camp-fires, showing that they will not return to their tents, you may know that they are determined to fight to the death.

The sight of men whispering together in small knots or speaking in subdued tones points to disaffection amongst the rank and file.

Too frequent rewards signify that the enemy is at the end of his resources; too many punishments betray a condition of dire distress.

To begin by bluster, but afterwards to take fright at the enemy's numbers, shows a supreme lack of intelligence.

When envoys are sent with compliments in their mouths, it is a sign that the enemy wishes for a truce.

a long time without either joining battle or taking themselves off again, the situation is one that demands great vigilance and circumspection.

If our troops are no more in number than the enemy, that is amply sufficient; it only means that no direct attack can be made. What we can do is simply to concentrate all our available strength, keep a close watch on the enemy, and obtain reinforcements.

He who exercises no forethought but makes light of his opponents is sure to be captured by them.

If soldiers are punished before they have grown attached to you, they will not prove submissive; and, unless submissive, then will be practically useless.

If, when the soldiers have become attached to you, punishments are not enforced, they will still be useless.

Therefore soldiers must be treated in the first instance with humanity, but kept under control by means of iron discipline. This is a certain road to victory.

If in training soldiers commands are habitually enforced, the army will be well-disciplined; if not, its discipline will be bad.

If a general shows confidence in his men but always insists on his orders being obeyed, the gain will be mutual.

chapter 10

Terrain

Sun Tzu said : We may distinguish six kinds of terrain, to wit:

(1) Accessible ground;

(2) entangling ground;

(3) temporizing ground;

(4) narrow passes;

(5) precipitous heights;

(6) positions at a great distance from the enemy.

Ground which can be freely traversed by both sides is called accessible.

With regard to ground of this nature, be before the enemy in occupying the raised and sunny spots, and carefully guard your line of supplies.

Then you will be able to fight with advantage.

Ground which can be abandoned but is hard to re-occupy is called entangling.

From a position of this sort, if the enemy is unprepared, you may sally forth and defeat him. But if the enemy is prepared for your coming, and you fail to defeat him, then, return being impossible, disaster will ensue.

When the position is such that neither side will gain by making the first move, it is called temporizing ground.

In a position of this sort, even though the enemy should offer us an attractive bait, it will be advisable not to stir forth, but rather to retreat, thus enticing the enemy in his turn; then, when part of his army has come out, we may deliver our attack with advantage.

With regard to narrow passes, if you can occupy them first, let them be strongly garrisoned and await the advent of the enemy.

Should the army forestall you in occupying a pass, do not go after him if the pass is fully garrisoned, but only if it is weakly garrisoned.

With regard to precipitous heights, if you are beforehand with your adversary, you should occupy the raised and sunny spots, and there wait for him to come up.

If the enemy has occupied them before you, do not follow him, but retreat and try to entice him away.

If you are situated at a great distance from the enemy, and the strength of the two armies is equal, it is not easy to provoke a battle, and fighting will be to your disadvantage.

These six are the principles connected with Earth. The general who has attained a responsible post must be careful to study them.

Now an army is exposed to six several calamities, not arising from natural causes, but from faults for which the general is responsible. These are: (1) Flight; (2) insubordination; (3) collapse; (4) ruin; (5) disorganization; (6) rout.

Other conditions being equal, if one force is hurled against another ten times its size, the result will be the flight of the former.

When the common soldiers are too strong and their officers too weak, the result is insubordination.

When the officers are too strong and the common soldiers too weak, the result is collapse.

When the higher officers are angry and insubordinate, and on meeting the enemy give battle on their own account from a feeling of resentment, before the commander-in-chief can tell whether or not he is in a position to fight, the result is ruin.

When the general is weak and without authority; when his orders are not clear and distinct; when there are no fixed duties assigned to officers and men, and the ranks are formed in a slovenly haphazard manner, the result is utter disorganization.

When a general, unable to estimate the enemy' s strength, allows an inferior force to engage a larger one, or hurls a weak detachment against a powerful one, and neglects to place picked soldiers in the front rank, the result must be rout.

These are six ways of courting defeat, which must be carefully noted by the general who has attained a responsible post.

The natural formation of the country is the soldier's best ally; but a power of estimating the adversary, of controlling the forces of victory, and of shrewdly calculating difficulties, dangers and distances, constitutes the test of a great general.

He who knows these things, and in fighting puts his knowledge into practice, will win his battles. He who knows them not, nor practices them, will surely be defeated.

If fighting is sure to result in victory, then you must fight, even though the ruler forbid it; if fighting will not result in victory, then you must not fight even at the ruler's bidding.

The general who advances without coveting fame and retreats without fearing disgrace, whose only thought is to protect his country and do good service for his sovereign, is the jewel of the kingdom.

The Art of War

Regard your soldiers as your children, and they will follow you into the deepest valleys; look upon them as your own beloved sons, and they will stand by you even unto death.

If, however, you are indulgent, but unable to make your authority felt; kind-hearted, but unable to enforce your commands; and incapable, moreover, of quelling disorder: then your soldiers must be likened to spoilt children; they are useless for any practical purpose.

If we know that our own men are in a condition to attack, but are unaware that the enemy is not open to attack, we have gone only halfway towards victory.

If we know that the enemy is open to attack, but are unaware that our own men are not in a condition to attack, we have gone only halfway towards victory.

If we know that the enemy is open to attack, and also know that our men are in a condition to attack, but are unaware that the nature of the ground makes fighting impracticable, we have still gone only halfway towards victory.

Hence the experienced soldier, once in motion, is never bewildered; once he has broken camp, he is never at a loss.

Hence the saying: If you know the enemy and know yourself, your victory will not stand in doubt; if you know Heaven and know Earth, you may make your victory complete.

chapter 11

The Nine Situations

Sun Tzu said : The art of war recognizes nine varieties of ground: (1) Dispersive ground; (2) facile ground; (3) contentious ground; (4) open ground; (5) ground of intersecting highways; (6) serious ground; (7) difficult ground; (8) hemmed-in ground; (9) desperate ground.

When a chieftain is fighting in his own territory, it is dispersive ground.

When he has penetrated into hostile territory, but to no great distance, it is facile ground.

Ground the possession of which imports great advantage to either side, is contentious ground.

Ground on which each side has liberty of movement is open ground.

Ground which forms the key to three contiguous states, so that he who occupies it first has most of the Empire at his command, is a ground of intersecting highways.

When an army has penetrated into the heart of a hostile country, leaving a number of fortified cities in its rear, it is serious ground.

Mountain forests, rugged steeps, marshes and fens - all country that is hard to traverse: this is difficult ground.

Ground which is reached through narrow gorges, and from which we can only retire by tortuous paths, so that a small number of the enemy would suffice to crush a large body of our men: this is hemmed in ground.

Ground on which we can only be saved from destruction by fighting without delay, is desperate ground.

On dispersive ground, therefore, fight not. On facile ground, halt not. On contentious ground, attack not.

On open ground, do not try to block the enemy's way. On the ground of intersecting highways, join hands with your allies.

On serious ground, gather in plunder. In difficult ground, keep steadily on the march.

On hemmed-in ground, resort to stratagem. On desperate ground, fight.

Those who were called skillful leaders of old knew how to drive a wedge between the enemy's front and rear; to prevent co-operation between his large and small divisions; to hinder the good troops from rescuing the bad, the officers from rallying their men.

When the enemy's men were united, they managed to keep them in disorder.

When it was to their advantage, they made a forward move; when otherwise, they stopped still. If asked how to cope with a great host of the enemy in orderly array and on the point of marching to the attack, I should say: "Begin by seizing something which your opponent holds dear; then he will be amenable to your will."

Rapidity is the essence of war: take advantage of the enemy's unreadiness, make your way by unexpected routes, and attack unguarded spots.

The following are the principles to be observed by an invading force: The further you penetrate into a country, the greater will be the solidarity of your troops, and thus the defenders will not prevail against you.

Make forays in fertile country in order to supply your army with food.

Carefully study the well-being of your men, and do not overtax them. Concentrate your energy and hoard your strength. Keep your army continually on the move, and devise unfathomable plans.

Throw your soldiers into positions whence there is no escape, and they will prefer death to flight. If they will face death, there is nothing they may not achieve. Officers and men alike will put forth their uttermost strength.

Soldiers when in desperate straits lose the sense of fear. If there is no place of refuge, they will stand firm. If they are in hostile country, they will show a stubborn front. If there is no help for it, they will fight hard.

Thus, without waiting to be marshaled, the soldiers will be constantly on the qui vive; without waiting to be asked, they will do your will; without restrictions, they will be faithful; without giving orders, they can be trusted.

Prohibit the taking of omens, and do away with superstitious doubts. Then, until death itself comes, no calamity need be feared.

If our soldiers are not overburdened with money, it is not because they have a distaste for riches; if their lives are not unduly long, it is not because they are disinclined to longevity.

On the day they are ordered out to battle, your soldiers may weep, those sitting up bedewing their garments, and those lying down letting the tears run down their cheeks. But let them once be brought to bay, and they will display the courage of a Chu or a Gui.

The skillful tactician may be likened to the shuai-ran. Now the shuai-jan is a snake that is found in the Chang mountains.

Strike at its head, and you will be attacked by its tail; strike at its tail, and you will be attacked by its head; strike at its middle, and you will be attacked by head and tail both.

Asked if an army can be made to imitate the shuai-ran, I should answer, Yes.

For the men of Wu and the men of Yue are enemies; yet if they are crossing a river in the same boat and are caught by a storm, they will come to each other's assistance just as the left hand helps the right.

Hence it is not enough to put one's trust in the tethering of horses, and the burying of chariot wheels in the ground.

The principle on which to manage an army is to set up one standard of courage which all must reach.

Thus the skillful general conducts his army just as though he were leading a single man, willy-nilly, by the hand.

It is the business of a general to be quiet and thus ensure secrecy; upright and just, and thus maintain order.

He must be able to mystify his officers and men by false reports and appearances, and thus keep them in total ignorance.

By altering his arrangements and changing his plans, he keeps the enemy without definite knowledge.

By shifting his camp and taking circuitous routes, he prevents the enemy from anticipating his purpose.

At the critical moment, the leader of an army acts like one who has climbed up a height and then kicks away the ladder behind him.

He carries his men deep into hostile territory before he shows his hand.

He burns his boats and breaks his cooking-pots; like a shepherd driving a flock of sheep, he drives his men this way and that, and nothing knows whither he is going.

To muster his host and bring it into danger: this may be termed the business of the general.
The different measures suited to the nine varieties of ground; the expediency of aggressive or defensive tactics; and the fundamental laws of human nature: these are things that must most certainly be studied.

When invading hostile territory, the general principle is, that penetrating deeply brings cohesion; penetrating but a short way means dispersion.

When you leave your own country behind, and take your army across neighborhood territory, you find yourself on critical ground.
When there are means of communication on

all four sides, the ground is one of intersecting highways.

When you penetrate deeply into a country, it is serious ground. When you penetrate but a little way, it is facile ground.

When you have the enemy's strongholds on your rear, and narrow passes in front, it is hemmed-in ground. When there is no place of refuge at all, it is desperate ground.

Therefore, on dispersive ground, I would inspire my men with unity of purpose.

On facile ground, I would see that there is close connection between all parts of my army.

On contentious ground, I would hurry up my rear.

On open ground, I would keep a vigilant eye on my defenses.

On ground of intersecting highways, I would consolidate my alliances.

On serious ground, I would try to ensure a continuous stream of supplies.

On difficult ground, I would keep pushing on along the road.

On hemmed-in ground, I would block any way of retreat.

On desperate ground, I would proclaim to my soldiers the hopelessness of saving their lives.

For it is the soldier's disposition to offer an obstinate resistance when surrounded, to fight hard when he cannot help himself, and to obey promptly when he has fallen into danger.

We cannot enter into alliance with neighboring princes until we are acquainted with their designs.

We are not fit to lead an army on the march unless we are familiar with the face of the country - its mountains and forests, its pitfalls and precipices, its marshes and swamps.

We shall be unable to turn natural advantages to account unless we make use of local guides.

To be ignored of any one of the following four or five principles does not befit a warlike prince.

When a warlike prince attacks a powerful state, his generalship shows itself in preventing the concentration of the enemy's forces.

Hence he does not strive to ally himself with all and sundry, nor does he foster the power of other states.

He carries out his own secret designs, keeping his antagonists in awe.

Thus he is able to capture their cities and overthrow their kingdoms.

Bestow rewards without regard to rule, issue orders without regard to previous arrangements; and you will be able to handle a whole army as though you had to do with but a single man.

Confront your soldiers with the deed itself; never let them know your design.

When the outlook is bright, bring it before their eyes; but tell them nothing when the situation is gloomy.

Place your army in deadly peril, and it will survive; plunge it into desperate straits, and it will come off in safety.

For it is precisely when a force has fallen into

harm's way that is capable of striking a blow for victory.

Success in warfare is gained by carefully accommodating ourselves to the enemy's purpose.

By persistently hanging on the enemy's flank, we shall succeed in the long run in killing the commander-in-chief.

This is called ability to accomplish a thing by sheer cunning.

On the day that you take up your command, block the frontier passes, destroy the official tallies, and stop the passage of all emissaries.

Be stern in the council-chamber, so that you may control the situation.

If the enemy leaves a door open, you must rush in.

Forestall your opponent by seizing what he holds dear, and subtly contrive to time his arrival on the ground.

Walk in the path defined by rule, and accommodate yourself to the enemy until you can fight a decisive battle.

At first, then, exhibit the coyness of a maiden, until the enemy gives you an opening; afterwards emulate the rapidity of a running hare, and it will be too late for the enemy to oppose you.

chapter 12

The Attack by Fire

Sun Tzu said : There are five ways of attacking with fire. The first is to burn soldiers in their camp; the second is to burn stores; the third is to burn baggage trains; the fourth is to burn arsenals and magazines; the fifth is to hurl dropping fire amongst the enemy.

In order to carry out an attack, we must have means available. The material for raising fire should always be kept in readiness.

There is a proper season for making attacks with fire, and special days for starting a conflagration. The proper season is when the weather is very dry; the special days are those when the moon is in the constellations of the Sieve, the Wall, the Wing or the Cross-bar; for these four are all days of rising wind.

In attacking with fire, one should be prepared to meet five possible developments:

(1) When fire breaks out inside to enemy's camp, respond at once with an attack from without.

(2) If there is an outbreak of fire, but the enemy's soldiers remain quiet, bide your time and do not attack.

(3) When the force of the flames has reached its height, follow it up with an attack, if that is practicable; if not, stay where you are.

(4) If it is possible to make an assault with fire from without, do not wait for it to break out within, but deliver your attack at a favorable moment.

(5) When you start a fire, be to windward of it. Do not attack from the leeward. A wind that rises in the daytime lasts long, but a night breeze soon falls.

In every army, the five developments connected with fire must be known, the movements of the stars calculated, and a watch kept for the proper days.

Hence those who use fire as an aid to the attack show intelligence; those who use water as an aid to the attack gain an accession of strength.

By means of water, an enemy may be intercepted, but not robbed of all his belongings.

Unhappy is the fate of one who tries to win his battles and succeed in his attacks without cultivating the spirit of enterprise; for the result is waste of time and general stagnation.

Hence the saying: The enlightened ruler lays his plans well ahead; the good general cultivates his resources.

Move not unless you see an advantage; use not your troops unless there is something to be gained; fight not unless the position is critical.

No ruler should put troops into the field merely to

gratify his own spleen; no general should fight a battle simply out of pique.

If it is to your advantage, make a forward move; if not, stay where you are.

Anger may in time change to gladness; vexation may be succeeded by content.

But a kingdom that has once been destroyed can never come again into being; nor can the dead ever be brought back to life.

Hence the enlightened ruler is heedful, and the good general full of caution.

This is the way to keep a country at peace and an army intact.

chapter 13

The Use of Spies

Sun Tzu said : Raising a host of a hundred thousand men and marching them great distances entails heavy loss on the people and a drain on the resources of the State. The daily expenditure will amount to a thousand ounces of silver.

There will be commotion at home and abroad, and men will drop down exhausted on the highways. As many as seven hundred thousand families will be impeded in their labor.

Hostile armies may face each other for years, striving for the victory which is decided in a single day.

This being so, to remain in ignorance of the enemy's condition simply because one grudges the outlay of a hundred ounces of silver in honors and emoluments, is the height of inhumanity.

One who acts thus is no leader of men, no present help to his sovereign, no master of victory.

Thus, what enables the wise sovereign and the good general to strike and conquer, and achieve things beyond the reach of ordinary men, is foreknowledge.

Now this foreknowledge cannot be elicited from spirits; it cannot be obtained inductively from experience, nor by any deductive calculation.

Knowledge of the enemy's dispositions can only be obtained from other men.

Hence the use of spies, of whom there are five classes:

(1) Local spies; (2) inward spies; (3) converted spies; (4) doomed spies; (5) surviving spies.

When these five kinds of spy are all at work,

none can discover the secret system. This is called "divine manipulation of the threads." It is the sovereign's most precious faculty.

Having local spies means employing the services of the inhabitants of a district.

Having inward spies, making use of officials of the enemy.

Having converted spies, getting hold of the enemy's spies and using them for our own purposes.

Having doomed spies, doing certain things openly for purposes of deception, and allowing our spies to know of them and report them to the enemy.

Surviving spies, finally, are those who bring back news from the enemy's camp.

Hence it is that which none in the whole army are more intimate relations to be maintained than with spies.

None should be more liberally rewarded. In no other business should greater secrecy be preserved.

Spies cannot be usefully employed without a certain intuitive sagacity.

They cannot be properly managed without benevolence and straightforwardness.

Without subtle ingenuity of mind, one cannot make certain of the truth of their reports.

Be subtle! be subtle! and use your spies for every kind of business.

If a secret piece of news is divulged by a spy before the time is ripe, he must be put to death together with the man to whom the secret was told.

Whether the object be to crush an army, to storm a city, or to assassinate an individual, it is always necessary to begin by finding out the names of the attendants, the aides-de-camp, and door-keepers and sentries of the general in command. Our spies must be commissioned to ascertain these.

The enemy's spies who have come to spy on us

must be sought out, tempted with bribes, led away and comfortably housed. Thus they will become converted spies and available for our service.

It is through the information brought by the converted spy that we are able to acquire and employ local and inward spies.

It is owing to his information, again, that we can cause the doomed spy to carry false tidings to the enemy.

Lastly, it is by his information that the surviving spy can be used on appointed occasions.

The end and aim of spying in all its five varieties is knowledge of the enemy; and this knowledge can only be derived, in the first instance, from the converted spy.

Hence it is essential that the converted spy be treated with the utmost liberality.

Of old, the rise of the Yin dynasty was due to Yi Zhi who had served under the Xia.

Likewise, the rise of the Zhou dynasty was due to Lu Ya who had served under the Yin.

Hence it is only the enlightened ruler and the wise general who will use the highest intelligence of the army for purposes of spying and thereby they achieve great results.

Spies are a most important element in war, because on them depends an army's ability to move.

고전 중의 고전인 손자병법은 한 번 읽고 밀쳐두는 책이 아니다. 또 한 번 읽어서 그 뜻을 제대로 이해하는 것조차 어렵다. 한자 원문을 우리말로 옮겨 놓은 것을 읽어도 그 뜻이 확실하게 들어오지 않는 경우도 많다. 그래서 뜻을 새기면서 읽어야 한다.

영어로 손자병법을 읽는 것은 손자가 펼치는 병법의 깊은 뜻을 새기는 새롭고 참신한 방법이다. 영어에는 우리말로 쓰인 한자어들보다 더 쉽고 의미가 분명한 단어들이 많다. 그래서 손자병법의 구절들을 영어로 읽으면서 우리말보다 영어가 더 쉽다는 생각을 자주 하게 된다.

병법에 능통하고 영어를 잘하는 데 공통적으로 필요한 것은 매일 규칙적으로 반복해서 읽고 뜻을 새겨서 입에서 술술 나오게 하는 것이다. 단지 이해하는 것으로 그치지 않고 그 참된 의미를 깨우쳐야 한다는 것이다.

옛날 천자문을 소리 내어 읽듯이 영어를 소리 내어 읽으면서 손자병법을 익히고 재미를 붙이면 손자병법도 영어도 자신의 삶이 되어 친숙하게 될 것이다.

배움은 익숙해지는 것이다. 익숙해지기 위해서는 함께 하는 시간이 많아져야 한다. 처음은 힘들어도 시간이 가면서 점점 쉬워진다. 여러분은 영어 손자병법을 통해서 병법을 통달하면서 영어에도 능통하게 될 수 있다.

또 영어와 병법을 통달해 나가는 과정을 통해서 여러분의 마음가짐이 달라지고 말과 행동도 달라질 것이다. 그래서 결국 여러분의 인생이 달라질 것으로 확신한다.

이용재

옛것은 많은 것을 말해준다

권선복
도서출판 행복에너지 대표이사

　손자병법은 고전 중에서도 으뜸으로 손꼽히는 고전입니다.

　전투에 승리하는 법을 그리고 있는 이 책은 장군들뿐만 아니라 많은 사람들에게 삶에 대한 영감을 주어 왔습니다.

　이는 손자가 적을 무찌르는 방법을 우리네 삶 속 여기저기에 적용시킬 수 있도록 전술을 예술의 경지로 한 단계 끌어올렸기 때문입니다.

　언제 굽히고 언제 쳐들어갈지 아는 손자병법은 '삶'이라는 치열한 전투를 치르기 위해 우리가 숙지해야 할 교재로 아슬아슬한 국제 외교를 할 때는 물론 한 개개인의 삶을 다가오는 미래 시대에 발맞추어 준비시키는 데에도 충분한 효력을 발휘할 것입니다.

　참으로 시의적절한 타이밍에 이 책이 나오게 되었습니다.

갈수록 복잡해지는 현대 사회에서 현대인들은 내외로 단단히 무장해야 합니다.

국가의 부흥을 위해서도 그렇고 스스로의 자기발전을 위해서도 그렇습니다.

지피지기면 백전불태이다. 적을 알고 나를 알면 백번 싸워도 위태롭지 않다. 손자병법의 명언입니다.

우리는 우리에 대해서 잘 알고 있고 적에 대해서도 잘 알고 있을까요?

삶을 살아가는 데 있어서 수억만 개 이상의 방법이 있을 것입니다. 그 모든 길을 하나하나 점검할 수는 없겠지만 훌륭한 고전에 의하여 성공적인 방법을 가늠할 수 있는 것은 축복이라 할 수 있겠습니다.

더군다나 한자로 된 원문을 영어로 다시 옮기고 해석하여, 영어적 표현을 자연스럽게 익히고 한자만 읽을 때 느껴지는 것과는 또 다른 묘미를 즐길 수 있을 것입니다.

독자 여러분들도 책을 읽으면서 적극적으로 현재 마주하고 있는 어려움을 풀기 위한 힌트로 삼을 수 있다면 더 바랄 나위가 없겠습니다.

부디 본 도서가 여러분의 꿈을 활짝 피우는 데 기여할 수 있기를, 그래서 행복하고 총명한 에너지가 팡팡팡! 터져서 삶이 기쁨으로 가득 차기를 기원합니다.

이것이 진정한 서비스다

이경숙 지음 | 값 20,000원

직무를 막론하고 '서비스 정신'이 '필수 요소'로 불리는 지금 이 시대, 버스, 택시 운전기사들에게 요구되는 서비스 정신에 대해서 자세히 다루고 있는 책이다. 버스, 택시 운전승무원들의 자존감을 높여 주는 한편 친절한 서비스 정신은 정확히 무엇이며, 어떻게 승객을 대해야 할지, 그리고 기사와 승객 모두가 행복해지는 win-win의 방법은 무엇인지 자세하게 망라하고 있는 것이 특징이다.

장기표의 행복정치론

장기표 지음 | 값 16,000원

2017년 발간된 『불안 없는 나라, 살맛나는 국민』의 개정판인 이 책은 전 인류의 문제를 해결하기 위해서 과거의 생산-소비적 관점을 과감히 포기하고 '자아실현'이라는 새로운 관점에서 인간의 행복을 정의해야 한다고 이야기한다. 특히 이윤 추구가 아닌 자아실현을 목표로 하는 시장경제와 그에 걸맞은 사회보장제도를 기반으로 하는 녹색사회민주주의를 주장하는 대목은 노동운동, 민주화운동의 선봉장 역할을 했던 저자의 경륜을 느낄 수 있다.

경찰을 말하다

박상융 지음 | 값 17,000원

우리가 미처 몰랐던 경찰 세계에 대한 방향을 제시해 주는 책인 동시에 한때 경찰이었던 저자가 통렬하게 느끼는 자기반성이 담겨있는 책이다. 사회정의의 최전선을 지키는 일선 경찰들의 애환을 그들의 시선에서 보는는 한편 '민중의 지팡이'가 민중에게 외면 받는 현실을 환기하고 개선을 촉구한다. 하지만 무엇보다 이 책이 소리 높여 말하고 있는 것은 현장을 지키는 경찰관들에게 가장 불합리한 경찰조직의 근본적 개혁이다.

아름다운 만남, 새벽을 깨우다

장만기 외 59인 지음 | 값 25,000원

이 책 '아름다운 만남, 새벽을 깨우다'는 한국인간개발연구원 창립 45주년을 맞아 연구원을 통해 새로운 인연을 맺고, 자신은 물론 뜻을 같이하는 사람들과의 연결과 발전을 경험한 60명 저자의 인생과 생각, 그리고 시대정신이 담긴 책이다. '인간개발연구원'이라는 이름 아래 모인 다양한 성별, 연령, 직업, 생각을 가진 사람들의 글을 통해 인간개발연구원이 지향하는 사회 비전과 선한 영향력을 한껏 느낄 수 있을 것이다.

조합의 건강이 농어촌의 미래다

정운진 지음 | 값 20,000원

본 도서는 농촌조합에서 근무한 경험을 바탕으로 저자가 느낀 조합의 폐단과 문제점을 생생하게 기록하면서 어떻게 하면 이를 개혁할 수 있을지 역설하고 있다. 잇따라 드러나고 있는 조합의 폐단에 대한 근본적 해결을 위해 전문경영인에게 실질적인 경영을 맡겨야 한다는 게 이 책의 핵심 주장이다. 또한 산재한 각종 단체의 통합과 조합의 농어촌 컨트롤 타워 기능 회복을 통해 농어촌의 발전 청사진을 제시하고 있다.

규소의 강력한 힘과 그 의학적 활용

이시형 · 선재광 지음 | 값 17,000원

독일, 일본 등지에서는 이미 건강을 지키는 중요한 미네랄의 일부로 받아들여지고 있으나 국내에서는 아직 생소한 '수용성 규소'의 존재와 그 효과를 알려주고 있는 책이다. 일본, 영국에서 규소수의 보조적 활용을 통해 난치병 환자를 치료한 사례와 함께 저자 선재광 한의학 박사가 직접 고혈압, 고지혈증 등의 환자들을 대상으로 규소수를 활용한 사례 등이 눈길을 끈다.

행복, 철들어 사는 재미

박종구 지음 | 값 15,000원

현대 사회를 살아가는 우리들에겐 나는 누구인지, 행복은 무엇인지, 삶은 무엇인가에 대해 진지한 성찰이 필요할 때가 있다. 『행복, 철들어 사는 재미』는 그런 소소한 진리에 대해서 담담하고 정갈하게 이야기한다. 잠시 목적 없는 삶을 멈추고 내 안을 지켜보며 나를 둘러싼 환경을 주시하기를 권하는 글을 읽어 내려가다 보면 작가가 전하는 소소한 진리에 대한 가치가 어느새 마음에 맴돌다 자리 잡을 것이다.

공부를 정복하라

서웅찬 지음 | 값 20,000원

어떻게 하면 공부를 잘할 수 있을까? 서울대 법대 출신 서웅찬 저자의 이 책은 대한민국에서 자랐다면 누구나 궁금해하는 '공부의 비법'을 매우 체계적이고 자세하게 알려주고 있는 책이다. 동기부여와 자신의 학습능력 파악, 공부계획 설정, 효율적 암기법과 노트필기법, 수험생에게 필요한 생활습관과 시험에 임박해서의 대처법까지 적극적인 실전 전략이 가득한 이 책은 시험을 앞둔 모든 이들에게 오아시스와 같은 존재가 될 것이다.

하루 5분, 나를 바꾸는 긍정훈련
행복에너지

'긍정훈련' 당신의 삶을
행복으로 인도할
최고의, 최후의 '멘토'

'행복에너지
권선복 대표이사'가 전하는
행복과 긍정의 에너지,
그 삶의 이야기!

인터파크
자기계발 분야 주간
베스트 1위

권선복 지음 | 15,000원

권선복

도서출판 행복에너지 대표
영상고등학교 운영위원장
대통령직속 지역발전위원회
문화복지 전문위원
새마을문고 서울시 강서구 회장
전) 팔팔컴퓨터 전산학원장
전) 강서구의회(도시건설위원장)
아주대학교 공공정책대학원 졸업
충남 논산 출생

책 『하루 5분, 나를 바꾸는 긍정훈련 - 행복에너지』는 '긍정훈련' 과정을 통해 삶을 업
그레이드하고 행복을 찾아 나설 것을 독자에게 독려한다.
긍정훈련 과정은 [예행연습] [워밍업] [실전] [강화] [숨고르기] [마무리] 등 총
6단계로 나뉘어 각 단계별 사례를 바탕으로 독자 스스로가 느끼고 배운 것을 직접
실천할 수 있게 하는 데 그 목적을 두고 있다.
그동안 우리가 숱하게 '긍정하는 방법'에 대해 배워왔으면서도 정작 삶에 적용시키
지 못했던 것은, 머리로만 이해하고 실천으로는 옮기지 않았기 때문이다. 이제
삶을 행복하고 아름답게 가꿀 긍정과의 여정, 그 시작을 책과 함께해 보자.

『하루 5분, 나를 바꾸는 긍정훈련 - 행복에너지』